The Sacraments:

Symbol, Meaning & Discipleship

Edited By
Andrew Bolton and Jane Gardner

Community of Christ

To purchase additional copies of this book, contact the publisher:
Herald Publishing House
P.O. Box 390
Independence, MO 64051-0390 USA
Phone: 1-800-767-8181 (toll-free) or (816) 521-3015
Canada: 1-800-373-8382 (toll-free)
Web site: *www.HeraldHouse.org*

10 09 08 07 06 05 5 4 3 2 1

ISBN 10 0-8309-1173-1
ISBN 13 978-0-8309-1173-8

Contents

Acknowledgments

Grateful appreciation is expressed for the skilled and sensitive writing contributed by Mary Jacks Dynes, Peter Judd, Kenneth McLaughlin, and Susan Skoor. Larry Tyree in his role as director of international resources has given much helpful feedback so that this book may bless the church worldwide. The above have also spent many hours in meetings helping shape this resource. Thanks are also gratefully extended to Danny Belrose, David Brock, Karen Freberg, and June Stephenson for their work on sample sacramental services.

We are also grateful for those across the church who reviewed the manuscript and gave helpful feedback: Danny Belrose, Don Compier, Amy Hamel, Doug and Christine Mack, Ruth Miluski, Randall Pratt, Susan Skoor, Art Smith, June Stephenson, Ann Winegarden, and Robert Wanga.

Steve McCrosson from Herald House and Jenn Killpack from the Communications Office have been most helpful. We are grateful to Jeff Piedmonte for his artistic giftedness in illustrating this resource.

—*The Editors*

Look especially to the sacraments to enrich the spiritual life of the body. Seek for greater understanding of my purposes in these sacred rites and prepare to receive a renewed confirmation of the presence of my Spirit in your experiences of worship.

—Doctrine and Covenants 158:11c

Preface

Sacraments have always had an important place in the practices of the Community of Christ. The monthly celebration of the Lord's Supper is among the highest-attended services of worship in many of the church's congregations. In this particular sacrament, disciples find strength and inspiration as they come together in unity to focus on Jesus Christ, who is the church's center and who calls them to follow him.

The sacraments of infant blessing, baptism, confirmation, ordination, and marriage are occasions when the candidate's family and church family join together in witness and support of those who enter into covenant with God.

The sacraments are acts of the assembled body that symbolize God's presence with the church and with each disciple. They are not separate from what the church is and what it does. Rather they are at the core of its ministries.

In this excellent resource the authors focus on how the sacraments connect the various elements of the church. The educational, worship, pastoral care, and outreach ministries of the church are, both separately and together, viewed as the context for God's love to touch lives through the sacraments.

We invite members and friends of the Community of Christ to read and study this resource. By doing so, their experience of the sacraments can be enriched and made more personal. Reflection on and participation in the sacraments are important disciplines in cultivating and strengthening one's relationship with the Divine. They can help individuals walk the path of the disciple more diligently and respond more generously to God's blessings in their lives.

May God's Spirit be felt more deeply by each one who shares in the sacraments of the church.

—The First Presidency

Chapter 1

Personal Stories of Sacramental Experiences

If you are new to sacraments perhaps these stories will suggest possibilities that will enrich your personal encounters with the Divine through sacraments such as baptism and Communion. If you have been blessed by participating in sacraments in the life of the church perhaps my stories will help you recall your own stories in whatever national or cultural context you live.

It was at a conference on community in Oxford, England, that I happened to sit down for the evening meal next to someone who turned out to be a Church of England bishop. In conversation he found out that I was a member of the Community of Christ. Before he began probing in detail the depth of my supposed heresies, I casually mentioned that we celebrated at least eight sacraments, one more than the Church of England or the Roman Catholic Church. Belonging to a Christian tradition that also valued the sacraments, the bishop was intrigued, the tone turned, and we continued in a delightful and warm conversation. Chatting about sacraments built a bridge to fellowship. Indeed, that is the awesome purpose of the sacraments: to build a bridge between people and God and with each other.

Community of Christ worship and covenantal life is sacramentally rich. When we perform the sacraments faithfully it is personally moving and deeply spiritual. The sacraments bless all who participate in them. If you ask people in our fellowship their most meaningful and memorable worship experience, it almost always involves sacraments. Yet the Holy Spirit has "yet more light and truth" to share with us as we seek greater understanding of these sacred rites:

> **Look especially to the sacraments to enrich the spiritual life of the body. Seek for greater understanding of my purposes in these sacred rites and prepare to receive a renewed confirmation of the presence of my Spirit in your experiences of worship. –Doctrine and Covenants 158:11c**

This is a promise of greater blessings.

Sacramental life begins in the great symphony of creation. I love the threads of interconnection in these prophetic words: "spirit and element, inseparably connected, receive a fullness of joy" (Doctrine and Covenants 90:5e). Our material world, nature, sings with the Spirit of the Creator. It is no accident that we choose to have our campgrounds in beautiful places: Dunfield, England; Tiona, Australia; Ziontario, Canada; or Samish Island, Camp Bountiful, and Happy Valley in the United States of Amer-

14

ica. These are just a few of the church's campgrounds where we sense the Spirit in and through God's creation, including the stirring of wind in trees, which evokes that deep spirit of peace in our souls. No cathedral or temple is more beautiful or more sacred.

Our campgrounds are sacramental as the Spirit dances, like sunlight on water, into our souls through nature. Every flower, bush, tree, and rock is alive with the glory of God if we had but eyes to fully see. In places like these I remember the story of creation, of how in the very beginning, the Spirit moved creatively on the face of the waters (Genesis 1:1). We are a people who worship the Divine amid God's awesome artistry. We lift our eyes to the hills or across the waters and understand more completely God's participation in the world.

Jesus is the first sacrament, for all things are created in and through him (John 1:1-4). It is in the story of Jesus that the Spirit becomes personal and human in a glorious way: full of grace and truth (John 1:14). If there is revelation of Creator through the sacrament of nature, then there is a fullness of divine revelation through the life, death, and resurrection of Jesus. Jesus is the window into God's light, the doorway into God's heart, the song sung out loud that is hummed in God's own soul. Jesus is the God story dramatized on the stage of human history in Roman-occupied Galilee and Judea. Jesus is the perfect translation of divine language into human talk and action. In Jesus, we see what God is like. We also glimpse what we can fully be as humans, for we are all created in the image of God.

All of the sacraments connect us in profound ways with the story of Jesus. And the connection is holistic—mind, body, emotions, and spirit—to all of God and the cause of Zion. Ordinary life becomes infused with new, extraordinary possibilities of healing and purpose through using gentle human touch, prayer, and simple gifts of nature: olive oil, bread, juice, and water.

Jesus was baptized to fulfill all righteousness (Matthew 3:15). I felt invited to follow. Baptism is the best decision I have ever made. At the age of twenty-two, I was immersed in tepid water on a January day in Penllergaer, South Wales, by Huw Evans. No one—not my parents, my friends, or my finest teachers—could choose for me to be a disciple of Jesus. It had to be my decision. How I agonized as I personally struggled through to the conviction that God was calling me to seek God's kingdom in this religious movement. Members of the congregation told me after I was baptized that the sun shone through the window and onto the water during the sacrament. I was buried with Christ and rose in newness of life, forgiven (Romans 6:3-4). I committed my whole self in that immersion in Christ, including my wallet.

The Spirit descended on Jesus like a dove after his baptism and I believe we can anticipate the same blessing. In the sacrament of confirmation, for the gift of the Holy Spirit, "spirit and element, inseparably connected" takes on new meaning (Doctrine and Covenants 90:5e). Elders laid hands on my head in prayerful encouragement and affirmation. They pointed to a Presence greater than I that would be available to lead and empower me on the path of the disciple. Many testify of becoming aware of the Holy Presence in that moment of prayer. For me that joyful awareness came some months later through witnessing someone else's baptism.

Bound together into sacred community through decision, baptism, and confirmation, we form the body of Christ in the world. We become the hands, feet, and voice of Jesus to our world, a revelation of divine purpose in a sinful, hurting, greedy, violent world.

I confess that I thought the Lord's Supper was boring when I was first baptized. It was not until I was working in Japan that my awareness began to deepen. Worship services in Japanese did not mean a lot to me even though the fellowship was always good and we were always made to feel so welcome. However, once a month, on Communion Sunday, we met again in an upper room. Although everything was still in Japanese, I knew the story and the Communion prayers. I found Communion speaking to me in new, deeper ways. I began to understand the sacraments as the international language of the church.

My colleague Jane Gardner tells of the time as a new elder when she received a call from a single mother requesting that she and her teenage daughter be able to share in the Lord's Supper. Was it OK to serve Communion "on demand"? Not sure how to respond she talked with the pastor. Together they decided it was the right thing to do. Later that afternoon the four of them met at the church. As the bread was served they all became aware of a powerful spirit of love. With tears in their eyes, the mother and daughter drank the juice. What the need was in that family Jane still does not know. But God knew, and they all experienced powerful reminders of the body of Christ broken as an act of love for us all.

In the marriage vows that I made to Jewell, my beautiful bride, the language was very clear. We both mutually agreed to be each other's companion for life. We made our covenant to each other before friends, family, and the Penllergaer congregation, where I was baptized. And we made our promises before God. It was the first time my parents had attended a Community of Christ worship service. My father was very moved, and we began healing from the alienation we felt when I left Catholicism to become a member of the Community of Christ. Reconciliation is part of every sacrament.

Baby blessings are a wonderful outreach ministry, as I discovered when we invited friends and colleagues to Matthew's blessing in the Old Bake House, Oxford, England. To my surprise almost everyone we invited came. Normally the congregation had twenty or thirty attending, but that day nearly ninety people crammed into the room. I was worried that we would not have enough chairs. My Uncle John, a Church of England vicar, shared in the service. Reed Holmes, Jewell's father, said the blessing prayer assisted by David Tucker. Poor baby Matthew cried and cried; not even Jewell could comfort him. Finally, I took Matthew and gave him my knuckle to suck. He quieted right down. In that moment, I understood the importance of my role as a father. There would be some needs in Matthew's life that only I could meet. I was called to be a father. Afterward, one of my fellow schoolteachers, a historian, said to a friend that he expected the Romans to burst in on this group of Christians at any moment. It was his way of saying that he had encountered something spiritually authentic. Another secular teacher friend commented, "It makes me want to go back to church."

The laying on of hands for the sick has brought many blessings. My sister-in-law Joy had cancer in both lungs two years ago. She and her husband were understandably anxious. We shared twice in the laying on of hands and a beautiful Easter service that brought great reassurance. The operation and treatment went so well. Joy recovered fully. Holy Spirit and skilled doctors together were instruments of healing. We are all grateful. Jesus still heals, whether body or spirit. The promise I am sure of is this: Come what may, the Spirit of Jesus will not leave or forsake us in life or in death.

My evangelist's blessing spoke words of great help and assurance to my soul as we met alone in the Llanelli church in South Wales. Counsel on choosing wisely whom I should marry, so that we could support each other in the cause of Zion, was timely and something I followed. The promise that God grants me a fresh and ever new beginning effectively silenced the unhelpful guilt that often stole my joy and peace of mind as a young adult. It was like having Jesus pray for me.

I have been ordained three times. Each calling has been confirmed in my soul and I have enjoyed a sense of direction and purpose in fulfilling each call.

There are other sacramental experiences in which we share. I shared in a beautiful hand-washing service a few years ago in Kirtland Temple. Foot washing is also sacramental. Funeral services can be sacramental as we celebrate the end of an earthly life and minister to each other in our sorrow. Giving for the work of the church and the cause of Zion is also sacramental. Living a life of stewardship, witness, peacemaking, and service is to live a sacramental life.

Reconciliation is potentially present in every sacrament. There is also a sacrament of reconciliation when two or more people put in the hard work to sort out difficulties, sometimes aided by another, according to the pattern in Matthew 18:15-22. Indeed, every sacrament has a peace and justice challenge. Baptism, for instance, is about burying and washing away our sins of violence, greed, and unfaithfulness, to rise out of the water committed to following the nonviolent Jesus, to become stewards, and to feed the hungry. In Communion we remember the Passover meal that became the first Lord's Supper and remember God's commitment to release people from economic slavery to economic justice. How can we feast at the Lord's Supper and not be concerned about the hungry in our world? We remember that Jesus suffered the death penalty at the hands of an occupying empire. We leave Communion called to commit ourselves to economic justice for all and the death penalty for none. To bless one child is to commit to creating a world that blesses every child. How can we celebrate and be blessed by beautiful nature at our campgrounds and be indifferent to pollution, gas-guzzling vehicles, and global warming?

We are so blessed in the Community of Christ by a rich sacramental tradition that connects our story to Christ's story in such a tangible way. I share a few stories to remind you of your sacramental blessings and also to witness of the promised blessings that await us all. Our task is to be the sacramental body of Christ to a hurting, needy world. Zion is the divine destiny of this world and the ultimate sacrament revealing God's purposes through creation and conversion. "Look especially to the sacraments to enrich the spiritual life of the body." Blessed as the body of Christ sacramentally, we are empowered to bless the world.

The following chapters are intended to help deepen your understanding of the power of the sacraments to mediate Christ's life through those who choose to follow him. In the following pages you are encouraged to discover deeper meanings of the sacraments. Practical suggestions are also made on how to practice the sacraments so they are beautiful and personally meaningful in the lives of those who celebrate and witness them. May you be blessed as you read.

Chapter 2

Sacraments as God's Self-Giving

Sacraments are means by which the church receives God's grace. They are tangible expressions of God's presence in the world. They are means whereby humans can catch some glimpse of the reality of God, who is ever near yet never fully known. In the sacraments, believers meet God in specific, unique ways. The sacraments embody aspects of the covenant that God makes with humanity. In these rites, humans sense the Holy.

Sacraments are ritual acts that are a regular part of the church's corporate worship. A ritual is an action that symbolizes a reality greater than what can be experienced directly. A sacrament consists of specific words and/or actions that have a recognizable constancy that endures.

To more fully understand the meaning of and possibilities for the sacraments we will begin our exploration by looking at the concepts that underlie the practices themselves.

The principle of sacrament has to do with God's self-revelation to the world—God's desire to be in relationship with creation. Sacrament assumes community that is created and sustained by God's gracious initiative. Without a belief that God chooses to be in relationship with creation, there is no sacrament or sacraments.

In understanding both the principle of sacrament and its specific expression in sacraments, it will be helpful to look at the primary ways God's self-revelation takes form. We will first affirm Jesus Christ as the most complete expression of God known to humanity. Then we will consider the church as gathered community and how it also is an essential expression of God. We then move to look at the ritual acts of the church as sacraments. Each of these expresses in tangible form what we might call the "higher order" sacramental expressions: Jesus Christ and the church.

Jesus Christ as the Primary Sacrament

Christians affirm that God's primary (most important) means of self-revelation is found in Jesus Christ. In him, we find the most complete revelation of God. In Jesus Christ, we know as much about God as can be known by humans. No other reality shows us God more fully than does the Son, whom God sent to be with us and show us the way.

In Jesus Christ, God came to live on earth as a human being—as one of us. We refer to this as *incarnation,* God in human form. If we as humans want to know about God, then we look to Jesus Christ, of whom the scriptures testify. Jesus affirmed this about himself when he said: "No one comes to the Father except through me. If you know me, you will know my Father also" (John 14:6). Here Jesus was talking not just about God, but rather about a particular relationship with God: that of loving Father and child.

Jesus Christ is therefore our most important means of knowing God. This enables us to proclaim Jesus Christ as the primary sacrament. He is "the way, and the truth, and the life" (John 14:6). It is through knowledge of and experience with Christ that we are brought close to God. It is through Christ that God accomplishes salvation for all who believe. It is Christ we seek to follow. We aim to become like him. This is the essence of what it means to do God's will.

The Church as Sacrament of Christ

We have access to Christ through the testimony of the scriptures and through our own experience with him, made possible by the Holy Spirit. Yet there is a sense in which we yearn for more. We envy those early disciples who knew Jesus in person and who walked with him in Palestine almost two thousand years ago. We anticipate his return as he promised after his resurrection.

After Christ's ascension, the community of his followers, who were left behind, formed the earliest Christian church. They gathered frequently to support each other through times of persecution and to celebrate their newly found faith. They shared together a common meal in memory of their Lord, as he had commanded them to do.

With Jesus no longer among them in person, they were held together and supported by each other and the promised comforter, the Holy Spirit. This sense of togetherness as the community of those who made the risen Christ their life focus sustained them. Through this church community their experience of Christ continued to be made real.

Writing only about a generation after Jesus' death and resurrection, the apostle Paul described the church as Christ's body. By using the metaphor of the physical body, Paul affirmed, "For just as the body is one and has many members, and all the members of the body, though many, are one body, so it is with Christ" (1 Corinthians 12:12). He went on to talk about both the unity and the diversity of the body and concluded with the declaration, "Now you are the body of Christ and individually members of it" (12:27).

In this sense, the community of those who follow Jesus—in other words, the church—becomes the tangible expression of who he is. The church, then, is sacrament of the One it is committed to follow. It is in the midst of the gathered community of the church that Christ is found. He is expressed in the unity that is created from all the diverse elements, the members who compose the body.

It may be possible to say that individuals who follow Christ personify him in their better moments. Yet such expressions are always secondary to what is found in the community of those who follow him. To say this does not claim perfection or superiority for the church. Rather it affirms that in our struggles to be faithful to his call, even in our imperfect response, Christ is found.

Within the church, Christ is expressed most directly in the people who assemble for worship. As believers express themselves in prayer and song they are sacrament of the One they proclaim and follow. Christ is present in this diverse body, rather than in any organizational structure or building.

The Sacraments as Acts of Christ's Body

The sacraments are the central actions of the assembled church. When the church gathers for worship it engages in sacramental acts that constitute the means of Divine-human interaction. These specific acts signify the broader, universal reality of God's desire to reach out in love toward all creation. They are gifts that God offers through the church, to be received by those who have faith. Sacraments are the tangible evidence of God's covenant relationship with creation.

The sacraments are both literal and symbolic. They use common, sensory elements (for example, hands, water, and bread) to express intangible reality. They involve words (in some cases specifically prescribed words) as well as well-defined actions. By receiving the sacraments, believers clasp the hand of God, who reaches toward them in covenant. They are blessed by the One whose life and work is blessing. The sacraments sustain, uplift, and heal. They symbolize God's gracious bridging of the rift created by human sin and extend the divine forgiveness that restores relationships.

Participation in the sacraments forms the character of the Christian believer as true and faithful disciple of Jesus Christ. The sacraments also shape the community of those who represent a foretaste of God's coming kingdom on earth, Zion. They connect today's church with those innumerable saints of earlier years, whose devotion is the bedrock of modern belief and practice. Likewise, they unite all those in any age who gather to profess belief in and commitment to their Lord across diverse geography and culture.

The early Christian church celebrated two sacraments: baptism and the Eucharist (Lord's Supper). Throughout the centuries, other symbolic actions came to be regarded as sacramental in various faith traditions. Today different denominations identify a variety of ritual acts as sacraments for their tradition.

The Community of Christ recognizes the following acts as sacraments: baptism, confirmation, the Lord's Supper (Communion), blessing of infants, ordination, marriage, administration for the sick (ministry of healing), and the evangelist's blessing.

The sacraments are essentially communal. Though they may have individual dimensions in their practice and application, they are never private; for the work of God in the lives of specific people is always for the good of the community. For this reason, most are celebrated in the setting of congregational worship. While their validity does not depend on this, the community context of the sacraments underscores the importance of relationships in the discipleship process. Their repetition in congregational life solidifies and strengthens the body.

All sacraments involve commitment and covenant. Several of the sacraments also mark the passage of life from birth to death. Shortly after birth, a child receives a blessing that symbolizes God's grace extended to each human being. On reaching the age of accountability (eight years), a child may be baptized to new life in Christ and confirmed a member of the church. In youth or adulthood, some people may be united in marriage and some may be ordained to priesthood responsibility. Although not identified as a sacrament of the church, a person's death may be ritualized in a funeral or memorial service.

Other sacraments may be provided at various times throughout a person's life: administration when a person is sick; the Lord's Supper as part of one's regular worship life in the congregation; the evangelist's blessing for times when one is in need of special guidance.

Together, the sacraments tangibly express the church's testimony that God is ever present and active in the life of each person. They demonstrate the covenant nature of the Divine-human relationship. Celebrated in the setting of the church, the sacraments provide the support of one's fellow disciples in community and remind the church of its focus.

Sacraments: Tangible Expressions of the Divine

GOD→	CHRIST→	CHURCH→	SACRAMENTAL→ ACTS	MISSION TO THE WORLD
			Baptism	
			Confirmation	
			Communion	
			Ordination	
			Laying on of Hands for the Sick	
			Marriage	
			Blessing of Children	
			Evangelist's Blessing	

Questions for Discussion

1. How would you explain the connection between sacrament and revelation? How is God revealed in the sacraments?

2. How do you find God revealed in Jesus Christ? In what ways is it meaningful to you to think of Jesus Christ as the primary sacrament?

3. Why is the concept of community so essential to our understanding of sacraments?

4. How do you see the church functioning as the sacrament of Christ? What does it mean to you to view the church as the "body" of Christ?

5. How does the church express the ministries of Jesus Christ? How do members of the church become "as Christ" to others?

6. How is the church assembled for worship "sacramental," that is, how does it reveal God?

7. How have you drawn closer to God through the sacraments of the church?

8. How do the sacraments serve to bring greater unity to the body?

9. How do the sacraments express the covenantal relationship between God and creation?

10. How has your faith been strengthened through the sacraments?

Chapter 3

Symbol, Ritual, and the Sacraments

Symbols and rituals are avenues for interacting with the Divine and with each other, particularly as we celebrate the sacraments of the church. Worship involving the sacraments is able to reach beyond the immediate realities of our lives. Everyday common symbols and rituals are used to embody God's presence in the world. "The sacraments are an extension of the ministry of incarnation in which God uses human nature and material things to express godliness tangibly in humankind" (*The Priesthood Manual*, 180). The awesomeness and mystery of God is made understandable to finite human beings in the gracious life of Jesus and through ordinary water, oil, and bread in the sacraments.

The linkage of spirit and element as articulated in 1833 by Joseph Smith Jr. provides a rich heritage of understanding the inseparable nature of physical and spiritual things: "The elements are eternal, and spirit and element, inseparably connected, receive a fullness of joy..." (Doctrine and Covenants 90:5e, adapted). And so in Communion, bread is not only physical food but also a spiritual feast. This is important because humans are physical and spiritual beings.

Symbols are actions or objects used to represent something else by association, resemblance, or convention. Symbols of faith are manifestations of the Divine using

- things (olive oil, water, bread),
- actions (laying on of hands),
- events (a Communion service),
- people (ministers or fellow disciples),
- communities (congregations), and
- symbolic language ("repent," "covenant," "consecrate," "bless").

The Nature of Symbols

The sacraments use physical objects and actions as symbols. Paul Tillich in *Dynamics of Faith* (New York: Harper and Row, 1957; 41-43), describes several characteristics of the nature of symbols.

1. *Symbols point beyond themselves to an unseen reality.* This is one characteristic that symbols have in common with signs: they are representational. For example, the stop sign at a crossroad points to the unseen requirement by law to stop the car before the intersection; as a faith symbol, the Communion bread represents Christ's body, now unseen.

2 *Symbols participate in the reality to which they point.* This characteristic
   sets symbols apart from signs. It is the nature of a symbol to go
   below the surface representation and make the unseen reality accessible. When we eat the Communion bread we remember and inter-
   nalize the story of Christ's sacrifice.

3 *Symbols open up levels of that reality that would otherwise remain closed.* This
   is difficult to intellectualize. We may come to "know" personally
   that the Communion bread is a symbol of Christ's sacrifice for us. It
   becomes a spiritual reality.

4 *Symbols unlock dimensions and elements of one's soul that correspond to the
   dimensions and elements of reality.* We are able to receive what symbols
   reveal to us in reality. In the Communion experience, because we
   "know" Christ died for us, our lives have the potential to be transformed. The symbol lives when the connection between bread as
   physical food and Christ as life-giving Spirit is clearly defined in the
   use and spoken meaning of the bread. Encountering Christ in this
   way we may feel led to live out our own discipleship in new and
   exciting ways.

Why do we need symbols? Religiously speaking, we are unable to express the infinite reality of God using direct language and objects because
they are finite. God transcends our understanding, and any attempt to
express the Divine in human terms must, by necessity, use symbols.

All sacraments involve symbols. These representations assist us
in connecting the ordinariness of everyday life with the Divine. The
symbols of laying on of hands, water, consecrated oil, bread, and wine
represent "unseen" realities that are sometimes difficult to express in
words. God uses these physical objects, actions, and symbolic language
to convey meanings that go far beyond what appears on the surface. They
represent something other than themselves. For example, repentance
from sin in baptism therefore is symbolized by the physical act of immersion in cleansing water.

Sacramental symbols convey the message that God is with us (Em-
manuel) and desires a continuing relationship with us. Through these
symbols, God becomes real and accessible, overcoming language barriers
and transcending the limits of our finite understanding.

Holistic Experience

Although it is difficult to quantify the power of interaction with the
Divine, worship that engages the whole person—rational, emotional, and
physical—has the greatest impact. When these dimensions of humanness
intersect in worship, communion with the Divine and with each other is

most often the result. "We respond physically, emotionally, intellectually, and socially because our response to God is total" (*The Priesthood Manual*, 180). Holistic experiences with the sacraments help us to comprehend God through a wider range of senses and emotions, rather than limiting our perceptions to rational ideas in our minds.

Some of the most powerful worship experiences center around the physical aspects of the sacraments, where touching, tasting, smelling, hearing, and seeing are all involved. Ministers lay hands on people for ordination, confirmation, an evangelist's blessing, and administration for the sick, symbolizing the power of God. Arms cradle babies for blessing. The use of cleansing water for baptism, consecrated oil for administration, and the broken bread and poured wine for Communion help us experience the holy in physical ways, involving the human body's five senses. Within the sacraments, when we combine the physical and spiritual with the emotional and rational aspects we stand as whole persons before God.

Ritual

A ritual involves any formal practice, custom, or procedure. Rituals knit our lives together, flowing through our days from birth to death. They can be as tiny as a phrase or gesture and as important as a cultural rite of passage for youth into adulthood. For example, a family may have an evening meal-time ritual of blessing the food and then launching into animated storytelling about the events of each person's day. Such rituals exist in households and communities and in each of us as individuals. In a religious context, rituals are special actions with prescribed form or order that have spiritual meaning. Sacred rituals provide sacramental and covenantal experiences linking God, individuals, and the community.

Sacraments are special sacred rituals with specific form and function. They have evolved over time through consistent recognition and appropriation of their sacred value. A sacrament is defined as "a Christian rite that is believed to have been ordained by Christ and that is held to be a means of Divine grace or to be a sign or symbol of a spiritual reality" (*The Priesthood Manual*, 178). The sacraments of the Community of Christ trace back to events in Jesus' ministry and Jewish tradition: baptism (Matthew 3:13-17; 28:18-20), confirmation (Matthew 3:11, Luke 3:16), Communion (Mark 14:22-25), laying on of hands (James 5:14-15, Mark 6:13), marriage (John 2:1-11 and Matthew 19:4-6), the blessing of children (Luke 18:15-17), ordination (Luke 6:12-16; 10:1), and the evangelist's blessing (John 17; Luke 22:31-32; Genesis 27:1-29). In some cases, the ritual acts associated with a sacrament are based on centuries of tradition (for example, using bread and wine for the Lord's Supper) while for others the procedure is evolving (for example, evangelist's blessings for congregations). In either case, the church's sacramental procedures are carefully specified. All sacraments are to be performed by priesthood members holding certain offices. Sometimes the words, actions, and form are prescribed. Recipients of some of the sacraments must meet certain qualifications. (See the latest editions of *The Priesthood Manual, Church Administrator's Handbook*, and the next chapter of this book for more information.)

Sacramental rituals can be described as ingrained habits that gather us and shape us as Christians. The sacraments are dramatic rituals involving personal covenant-making, God's presence, and community commitment that quite significantly result in changes to people's lives. The symbolic drama of the sacraments is, in a sense, the Word made visible. The gospel comes alive. Our participation also goes beyond ourselves and conveys the meaning of the gospel to others who are present. When participation in the sacraments becomes habitual, without commitment and change in our lives, it is nothing more than an empty ritual—we merely go through the motions. Inherent in each of the sacraments is the necessity that there will be a change in understanding, attitude, and behavior by the worshiper.

Experiencing the Divine in sacramental ritual lays claims on our lives—the gospel becomes a part of us, and we become a part of it. We become committed to God, as God is committed to us. In the process, we become committed to each other. This is no small matter. Through the sacraments we participate in the gospel, individually and corporately, as well as proclaim it. The celebration of the sacraments is at the core of our Christian identity and the church's mission to build zionic communities.

Corporate Acts

The sacraments, by their nature, are functions of the fellowship of the church. They are specific actions of the gathered "body"—the body of Christ—and are basic to corporate Christian life. Because of this, most sacraments are celebrated in a congregational worship setting. In this venue, the assembled church represents the covenant community and participates fully in the sacred ritual. In a baby blessing, for example, those present affirm their willingness to provide love, support, and guidance to the growing child and his or her immediate family and caregivers. They may also remember similar sacramental moments in their lives or in the life of the congregation. In essence, the sacrament causes the community to recall, remember, and recommit their lives. Without this corporate involvement, the sacrament is incomplete. Thinking that sacraments are between "God and me" negates the powerful relational base of the Christian community. When sacraments involve individuals making personal covenants, there is also an effect on the entire community—the family of the blessed baby can expect the congregation to provide nurturing, training, and love because of the corporate dimension of the sacrament.

Janet R. Walton in the book *Art and Worship* lists five human needs in the people assembled for sacramental worship (The Liturgical Press, 1991; 55-67). They can be developed as follows:

1. *Transcendence*

The sacraments transcend immediate realities. We need to experience wonder and awe. In sacramental ritual, we are filled with a sense of tremendous mystery and, at the same time, an awareness that God desires to participate in our lives.

2. *Connection*

Through the sacraments we are connected to centuries of Christian ritual. We have a sense of heritage and amazing linkage to those Christians who have served before us. We also are connected through the celebration of sacramental rituals within our congregations as the body of Christ.

3. *Beauty*

Beauty has many definitions. In this context, beauty encompasses more than what is pleasing—it includes what is truthful and original. In the sacraments, beauty is often found in the connection between symbols and the realities of life. The sacraments convey a unique sense of beauty and richness that points not to the acts themselves but to the beauty and richness of life itself. The truth they represent is powerful and communicates something of the beauty and powerful nature of God.

4. *Affirmation*

In sacramental ritual we feel affirmation of God's love for us and, in turn, express that love by affirming the worth of others.

5. *Faithfulness*

Through the sacraments we feel God's limitless grace for us. God's faithfulness is beyond our understanding and expectations. In response, we are called to faithfulness, remembering the purpose of our discipleship and our commitment to struggle together along the path of the disciple.

The sacraments do not exist for the benefit of the church but rather for the benefit of the world. Sacramental rituals sustain the church and its members for the express purpose of being empowered to reach out to others.

Living Sacramentally

Discussion of the sacraments can be broadened to include the concept of living sacramentally.

> All acts of worship are by nature and intent sacramental; that is, they serve as a means for Divine-human encounter. A sacramental experience, of course, is not limited to corporate or private acts of worship. One can have a sacramental experience watching a sunset, hearing a bird sing, or driving through the mountains. —*The Priesthood Manual*, 177

Viewing the world sacramentally is to see the divine Incarnation in the midst of our daily activities—God-in-Christ is with us. The sacramental rituals of the church spill over into recognizable patterns in the world. In her article "Everyday Sacraments," Barbara Brown Taylor describes it this way:

> The same pattern of rebirth that I learned in baptism showed up in everything from bathing to watering plants. The same pattern of relationship that I learned in communion was available in every meal eaten mindfully. The laying on of hands took place as I held a crying baby or rubbed the shoulders of a tired friend. When I walked outside and looked at the smoking compost heap, I saw a sacrament of death turning into life. When I used my little bottle of white-out [eraser] to correct a mistake, I remembered that my errors did not have to be permanent. Everywhere I turned, the most insignificant things in the world were preaching little sermons to me. Everywhere I turned, the world was leaking light. All that was required was my willingness to walk through the world aware of God's presence, ready to hold ordinary things up to heaven with my own hands so that I and anyone else who was interested could see the holiness in them—even the soiled and broken things that were just waiting for someone to come along and love them. —*The Living Pulpit* (July/September 2003)

In other words, living sacramentally is experiential; it occurs, as Tillich noted, "when the spiritual breaks in on the temporal and the temporal is prepared to receive it." It encompasses all of life. How could sacramentally living the four weeks of Advent affect our understanding of "waiting" and "preparation"? How different might the six-week period of Lent before Easter be if we approached it sacramentally? A sacramental journey involves spiritual discipline, education, and discernment.

Conclusion

Sacraments are not other-worldly exercises. They use symbol and ritual to convey the message of incarnation—the embodiment of the Word. They are down-to-earth and involve everyday objects, actions, and language, making them accessible to everyone who is a disciple of

Jesus Christ. As a congregation, we meet in worship confident that the transcendent God will be present and bless our preparation. Through the sacraments we make ourselves available to God and to each other. Participating in the sacraments gives us a sense of individual interaction with the Divine as well as a corporate sense of stewardship over the world. As we go forth from the sacraments, we leave as changed people, assured of God's grace, ready to live sacramental lives and empowered to share our witness and resources with others.

> To you who hear my voice and know my promises I will reveal myself and give my peace, even in the midst of your uncertainties. Indeed, I am longing to pour out greater blessings than you have ever known if you, my people, will open yourselves through preparation, study, and prayer. Look especially to the sacraments to enrich the spiritual life of the body. Seek for greater understanding of my purposes in these sacred rites and prepare to receive a renewed confirmation of the presence of my Spirit in your experiences of worship. —Doctrine and Covenants 158:11a-c

Questions

1. What are some of the symbols found in a confirmation? rituals?

2. Why do worshipers find the sacraments memorable and meaningful?

3. How is the principle of incarnation demonstrated through the sacraments?

4. How can the celebration of the sacraments be more than blind repetition and habit?

5. Why is the congregation's participation vital in the celebration of most of the sacraments?

6. When have you experienced a sacramental moment in your daily journey (not in a worship service)?

7. How do the sacraments "enrich the spiritual life of the body" (Doctrine and Covenants 158:11c)?

8. How does participation in a sacrament aid the follower of Jesus in conversion or personal transformation?

9. On page 32 in the section on ritual a number of scriptures are used to illustrate how the sacraments are rooted in the ministry of Jesus and the life of the early church. An exercise that might be helpful would be to complete the following table by looking up the scriptures and seeing how a sacrament has developed from the scriptures referenced and its meaning:

Sacrament	Scripture	Development and Meaning
Baptism	Matthew 3:3-17 Matthew 28:18-20 John 3:1-8 Acts 8:35-38 Romans 6:1-4	
Confirmation	Matthew 3:11 John 3:1-8 Luke 3:16 Acts 2:1-18 Acts 8:44-47	
Communion	Luke 22:14-20 Luke 24:28-31 Mark 14:22-25 I Corinthians 11:23-32	
Ordination	Luke 6:12-16, 10:1 Acts 13:1-3	
Marriage	John 2:1-11 Matthew 19:4-6	
Blessing of Children	Luke 18:15-17	
Laying on of Hands for the Sick	Mark 6:13 James 5:14-15	
Evangelist's Blessing	John 17 Luke 22:31-32 Genesis 27:1-29	

Chapter 4

Sacraments in the Church

You have already been told to look to the sacraments to enrich the spiritual life of the body. It is not the form of the sacrament that dispenses grace but it is the divine presence that gives life. Be respectful of tradition and sensitive to one another, but do not be unduly bound by interpretation and procedures that no longer fit the needs of a worldwide church. In such matters direction will come from those called to lead. —Doctrine and Covenants 162:2d

Universals and Particulars in the Sacraments

Universals and particulars can be identified in disciplines as diverse as philosophy, architecture, and creative writing. While the concept of universals and particulars is not unique to the study of the eight sacraments celebrated in the Community of Christ, it provides a helpful framework for this discussion of the sacraments.

A **universal** applies, describes, or refers to the whole of a subject or category. Universals in the sacraments are spiritual characteristics or eternal qualities that are repeatable and remain unchanged in the midst of changeable situations. A **particular** applies, describes, or refers to a specific, distinct, or portion of a subject or category. Particulars in the sacraments are specific, changeable expressions of a universal in the context of the celebration of a sacrament.

Perhaps a simpler way to state this when speaking of the sacraments is as follows: the universal is the broad principle that is being brought to life by the sacrament, and the particulars are the rituals or practices that enact this broad principle. Thus, even though different Christian faith communities celebrate the sacraments through diverse particulars, the universals may well be identical.

Sacramental universals include the following:
- Connection to God and all of God's creation
- Interaction between humanity and God
- Connection to past, present, and future generations of God's people
- Recognition of God's grace and saving activity among us
- Acknowledgment of the Holy in the midst of the ordinary
- Covenanting between humans and the Divine and the Divine with humans

Sacramental particulars include the following:
- The prescribed ritual, act, or procedure to be followed when celebrating a sacrament (for example, kneeling for Communion prayers, laying on of hands, anointing with oil, immersing in water)
- Physical objects or emblems to be used in the ritual (for example, olive oil, water, bread, juice)
- Prescribed words or prayers (for example, Communion prayers, baptismal statement, marriage vows)

No discussion of the sacraments is complete without recognizing the existence of both universals and particulars. The sacraments are most fully described by looking at both. Moreover, both universals and particulars are important. They complement one another. However, while particulars are important, universals are *more* important. Throughout the ages Christians, including disciples within the Community of Christ, have spent so much time and energy on the particulars that they fail to grasp and fully honor the timeless universals found in the sacraments. Recognizing universals allows us to appreciate the sacraments with our brothers and sisters of other faiths. Countless hours have been spent extolling the virtues of Community of Christ rituals and criticizing the particulars of other faith communities, without recognizing the underlying universals that bring vitality and meaning to all the sacraments.

A classic example of this point is when a candidate for baptism is immersed (a particular tradition of the Community of Christ) but the candidate's nose does not go completely under the water. While the intent of the particular has been fulfilled and the universal has been honored, some would claim the ritual to be so flawed as to lack effectiveness. Does the candidate need to be reimmersed? Does the particular override the universal? Can zealous compliance with particulars become legalistic? Or is the universal only fully understood if the particular is accurately carried out?

While both universals and particulars are important in the consideration of the sacraments, the scope of the universal is, by definition, broader and less bound by time and culture. However, the universal standing alone, without the particular, cannot be put into practice in a way that permits the power of symbol, action, and holy repetition to be experienced by humans.

Particulars, by their nature, are changeable over time. They have no meaning outside the meaning assigned to them by each generation of believers and disciples. The changing of a particular is a matter to be taken seriously by the faith community. It should be accomplished in conformity with established procedures, but it is not a task to be avoided or declared outside the scope of responsibility of the church. Indeed, the changing of a particular is often inextricably linked to a broadening of the understanding of an underlying universal.

When the Community of Christ changed from a "close" to "open" position on the serving of the Lord's Supper, there was not only a change in the ritualistic particular, but also a broader understanding of the universals of Communion. Another recent example is the contemporary language revisions to the Communion prayers (see appendix).

Losing sight of the universals in the sacraments is ecclesiastically dangerous. It leads to the idolatry of form and procedure rather than the rightful focus on purpose and meaning. Losing sight of the particulars in the sacraments leads to disregard of tradition and a dilution of the shared experience of the ages.

Particulars of Community of Christ Sacraments

By their nature particulars change and evolve. Refer to the latest version of the *Church Administrator's Handbook* and the church's Web site (*www. CofChrist.org*) for the most recent documentation on Community of Christ sacramental particulars.

Priesthood and Sacraments

There are two priesthoods, the Melchisedec and the Aaronic. Within these priesthood orders there are several offices, each with special functions and ministries to perform....

The early verses of chapter 7 of the letter to the Hebrews refer to Melchisedec, and he is presented as resembling the ministry of Jesus Christ. Thus, Melchisedec was seen by the Jewish tradition as a model for the Jewish priesthood and by the Christian tradition as a prefiguring of the ministry of Jesus Christ.... The Aaronic priesthood includes a Christian form of the Levitical ministries described in the Old Testament. It was named after Aaron who was ordained to this responsibility under the hands of Moses.*

The offices of the Aaronic priesthood are deacon, teacher, and priest. The priest can ordain, baptize, and administer Communion. The offices of the Melchisedec priesthood are elder, seventy, high priest, bishop, evangelist, apostle, and president. Melchisedec priesthood can officiate in all the sacraments with the exception of the evangelist's blessing, which is only given by those holding the office of evangelist. While there is a diversity of office and function there is an equality of calling and dignity in each office.

The Priesthood Manual (Herald House, 2004)

The Community of Christ recognizes the following eight sacraments:

1 - Baptism

Baptism is the recognized act of commitment to Christian discipleship. In the tradition of the Community of Christ, the combined acts of baptism and confirmation constitute entrance not only into the larger Christian fellowship, but also into denominational membership.

The prerequisites for baptism are found in the Doctrine and Covenants.[1] Candidates for baptism must be eight years of age or older. They should be properly instructed in Christian discipleship, with the instruction appropriate to the candidate's age and capacity to comprehend. Instruction may be both before and after the baptism.[2] All baptisms are to be approved in advance by the pastor.[3, 4, 5]

Baptism should occur within the context of a specially planned service of worship, and be held either in a facility equipped with a baptismal font or equivalent, or outdoors in a safe and appropriate body of water.

Aaronic priests or Melchisedec priesthood members perform baptisms. There should be only one officiating minister unless the candidate's size or health dictates otherwise. Baptisms within the Community of Christ are by bodily immersion. The minister is to use the words prescribed by the Doctrine and Covenants: "…[C]alling him or her by name: Having been commissioned of Jesus Christ, I baptize you in the name of the Father, and of the Son, and of the Holy Ghost, Amen."[6] Church tradition recognizes the use of the word "Spirit" instead of "Ghost" but no other word substitutions.

Rebaptism is provided only for members who have been expelled from the church and is permitted after approval of the pastor, mission center president, field apostle, and First Presidency, with the authorization of the Standing High Council.

2 - Confirmation

Confirmation is the second portion of the entrance into membership in the Community of Christ. It consists of a prayer offered by one of two officiating ministers, both of whom place their hands on the head of the candidate. Only members of the Melchisedec priesthood perform confirmation.

The prayer of confirmation acknowledges the presence of God through the Holy Spirit in the life of the candidate. The prayer should include recognition of membership status within the Community of Christ and often contains words of blessing, encouragement, and counsel.

Confirmation is linked to baptism by water. The two sacraments should be performed without great time lapse between the two. Even so, it is preferable for the two sacraments to be celebrated in two separate worship experiences, giving focus to the particular meaning of both. Separation in time also provides for the encouraging and instruction of new members (see endnote 2).

3- Communion

Communion (often called the Lord's Supper or, especially in other faith communities, Eucharist) is the act of partaking of bread and wine in symbolic remembrance of the life, teachings, death, and resurrection of Jesus Christ. The act is to conform to the established practices of the church and is traditionally celebrated on the first Sunday of the month, but it may be held more frequently as circumstances dictate.

The sacrament is normally held in the context of a public worship service and is often preceded by a Communion message or statement. Moreover, it is tradition that an offering for the benefit of the poor and needy (oblation) be collected at a Communion service. Aaronic priests and Melchisedec priesthood members offer the Communion prayers and serve the emblems.

The sacrament consists of the prayers of blessing on the bread and wine[7] (see also the appendix for contemporary language versions) as the participants kneel, followed by the eating of a small portion of sacramental bread and drinking a sip or two of sacramental wine.

Communion wine should be unfermented grape juice, water, or a culturally appropriate substitute where grapes are not readily available.[8, 9, 10] The grape juice and bread may be either homemade or commercially prepared.

Bread and wine used in the sacrament are blessed for those who partake of it at the time of the service and with the understanding of its purpose. The blessing does not relate to later use and does not change the elements or composition of the bread or wine.[11]

All committed Christians are free to participate in the sacrament as offered in the Community of Christ. The serving ministers should not attempt to determine who should or should not partake. The decision is left to the participant. Children of family members within the Community of Christ should not partake until such time as they are baptized and confirmed.

The Communion emblems may be served either at the same time (provided both prayers of blessing have been offered, or the new combined Communion prayer has been said) or one after the other. Ordained and unordained persons may prepare the emblems, set the Communion table, remove any covering linens, and handle the emblems and serving items.

The Communion prayers are to be offered using the words traditionally prescribed in Doctrine and Covenants 17 or the contemporary language versions (see appendix).

When taking the Communion emblems to persons not able to be at the worship service, prayers of blessing on the bread and wine may be repeated, but that is left to the discretion of the presiding minister.

4- Ordination

Two members of the priesthood authorized to ordain men and women to the specific office traditionally perform the sacrament of ordination to priesthood. The sacrament is performed as a prayer, with the officiating ministers placing their hands on the head of the ordinand. The prayer pronounces the ordination and office, and it is often a statement of thanksgiving, counsel, and blessing. Ordination occurs in the setting of a planned service of worship in which this sacrament is the focal worship element. The officiating ministers are selected through consultation between the ordinand and the supervising administrative officer.

Aaronic priests and Melchisedec priesthood members may officiate at the ordinations of members of the Aaronic priesthood, and high priests and elders at the ordination of elders. High priests may be ordained by other high priests, including bishops and evangelists. Members of the Council of Twelve or First Presidency or their designee normally ordain evangelists or bishops, with any high priest eligible to assist. A member of the First Presidency, Council of Twelve, or Council of Presidents of Seventy normally ordains to the office of seventy, with any other high priest or seventy assisting.

The officiating minister should ensure that the ordination is reported immediately to the Office of Membership Records so that the ordinand receives a priesthood license, certifying the person as an ordained minister.

For information related to priesthood calls, expectations, review, and status, see the most recent *Church Administrator's Handbook*.

5- Laying On of Hands for the Sick

Any person who suffers spiritual, emotional, or physical illness may request that the elders of the church offer a sacramental prayer, anointing him or her with oil in the name of the Lord (see James 5:14). The prayer is accompanied by the laying on of hands and is often spoken of as "administration." The sacrament may be performed publicly in the context of worship, but it is usually performed in the privacy of a home, hospital room, or quiet area of the church. Two members of the Melchisedec priesthood customarily perform it, although one elder or three may participate. The sacrament may be preceded by brief periods of counsel or pastoral comfort. However, the sacrament itself consists of anointing the head with consecrated olive oil, the anointing statement, and the prayer of confirmation.

Traditionally, one elder anoints with consecrated oil and places his or hands on the head of the person while praying briefly the anointing statement. The second elder then joins the first in placing his or her hands on the person's head while offering a prayer of confirmation.

Sufficient olive oil should be used in anointing for it to be felt, but only one or two drops are required. Anointing should be on the top of the forehead area. Anointing of other body parts is not part of the sacramental procedure.

Family members and loved ones may join the elders in surrounding the person's bedside or chair.

To consecrate olive oil the cap should be removed from the vial or bottle and a prayer offered by a member of the Melchisedec priesthood. Oil should not be consecrated in large quantities then divided into smaller portions and distributed. No church law or tradition authorizes the use of consecrated oil by those who are not elders. The consecrated oil is not considered curative or medicinal itself, rather acts as a symbol of healing.

6-Marriage

Marriage is traditionally defined as a sacred covenant between a man and a woman seeking to make a lifelong commitment of mutual support, love, and faithfulness to one another. The marriage sacrament is usually celebrated in a public wedding ceremony held in a church facility or other appropriate site. The ceremony is a carefully crafted service of worship planned in the context of premarital counseling offered by the officiating minister or designee. Aaronic priests and Melchisedec priesthood members are eligible to perform a wedding ceremony, subject to any legal restrictions of the governmental jurisdiction in which the wedding is to occur and subject to the scope of authority given to them by the church.

While the structure and degree of formality of the wedding service will vary according to local custom and personal preference, the sacrament as celebrated in the Community of Christ should be in harmony with the Doctrine and Covenants.[12] Thus, during the exchange of vows, the couple should be asked, "Do you both mutually agree to be each other's companion, husband and wife, observing the legal rights belonging to this condition; that is, keeping yourselves wholly for each other, and from all others, during your lives?" After answering in the affirmative, the officiating minister pronounces the couple married, and offers a blessing such as the following: "May God add his blessings and keep you to fulfill your covenants from henceforth and forever. Amen"

At the conclusion of the wedding service, it is the responsibility of the officiating minister to assure compliance with all the legal reporting and recording requirements of the local governmental jurisdiction.

In some nations, a corresponding civil ceremony is conducted by government officials.

7 - Blessing of Children

Jesus called for children to be brought to him for special attention and blessing. In that tradition, the church continues to provide for a sacramental prayer offered on behalf of infants and young children.

The sacrament consists of a prayer. It is to be offered by a member of the Melchisedec priesthood. Tradition calls for the parents to bring the child forward, and for one elder to hold the child, if small, while another elder places his or her hands on the child and offers the prayer of blessing. The parents often stand next to the officiating elders. If the child is older, a parent who is seated in a chair may hold him or her, or the child may sit alone in the chair. The sacrament is often performed within the child's first few weeks of life, although it may be performed for an older child, up to the child's eighth birthday.[13] As a child approaches the age of eight, it is more appropriate to focus on preparing the child for baptism rather than to provide for a sacramental blessing.

There is no required formula for the prayer, but it is appropriate to include a statement of thanksgiving, blessing, recognition of the importance of family and friends in the nurture of the child, and recognition of the role of the congregation in instructing and supporting the child.

The blessing of a child is traditionally a public event held in the context of a congregational worship service specially planned for that purpose, but other settings may be provided for. The pastor is to be sensitive to parents who wish for a child to be blessed on a specific day, balancing the need for enough planning time with the wishes of the family.

The blessing is not a part of the baptismal sacrament or entrance ritual into the denomination. Any child is a candidate for blessing.

8- Evangelist's Blessing

The evangelist's blessing (formerly called patriarchal blessing) is a prayer (usually recorded and transcribed) offered by a member of the Order of Evangelists. It is performed in a home, chapel, or other appropriate site. The blessing is not held in the context of a public worship experience. The blessing is performed by one evangelist, who places his or her hands on the head of the candidate and delivers words of thanksgiving, affirmation, counsel, life direction, and blessing. Before the blessing, the evangelist and candidate arrange to meet for conversation and instruction. Any person eight years of age or older is a candidate for the sacrament, although the blessing is rarely offered for someone who has not reached adolescence.

A copy of the recorded prayer may be provided to the candidate.

In addition to the sacrament, evangelists may be called on to offer special prayers of blessing for individuals, families, and congregations. The evangelist works within guidelines provided by the Order of Evangelists in giving this specialized ministry.

Study Questions

1. Name two universals of the sacrament of blessing of children. Name two particulars.
2. When does a denomination have the right—or even the obligation—to alter the particulars of a sacrament in order for the universals to be more clearly honored?
3. What does Doctrine and Covenants 162:2 have to say on the subject of universals and particulars?
4. The authors state that both universals and particulars are important but that universals are more important. Do you agree?
5. What is the broader understanding of the universals of the Lord's Supper referred to by the authors?
6. If a congregation decided to celebrate the Lord's Supper every Sunday, what would change—particulars or universals?
7. How do the contemporary language and combined Communion prayers exemplify changes in sacramental particulars? How do the language changes help or hinder your worship?
8. If the particular necessitating rebaptism for Community of Christ membership were discontinued in the future, what changes would this indicate in the understanding of the universal that undergirds baptism? How might the particulars be changed?
9. Can you think of some particulars of the sacraments that are unique to your congregation?

Notes

Doctrine and Covenants and World Conference Resolutions (WCR)

1. Doctrine and Covenants 17:7a–d
   And again by way of commandment to the church concerning the manner of baptism: All those who humble themselves before God and desire to be baptized, and come forth with broken hearts and contrite spirits, and witness before the church that they have truly repented of all their sins, and are willing to take upon them the name of Jesus Christ, having a determination to serve him to the end, and truly manifest by their works that they have received of the Spirit of Christ unto the remission of their sins, shall be received by baptism into his church.

2. Doctrine and Covenants 17:18a–c
   The duty of the members after they are received by baptism: The elders or priests are to have a sufficient time to expound all things concerning the church of Christ to their understanding, previous to their partaking of the sacrament, and being confirmed by the laying on of the hands of the elders; so that all things may be done in order. And the members shall manifest before the church, and also before the elders, by a godly walk and conversation that they are worthy of it, that there may be works and faith agreeable to the Holy Scriptures, walking in holiness before the Lord.

3. Doctrine and Covenants 120:4a
   In both branches and districts the presiding officers should be considered and respected in their offices;

4. Doctrine and Covenants 125:14a–c
   Branches and districts are to be conducted according to the rules given in the law as directed in a former revelation: They shall take the things which have been given unto them as my law to the church to be my law to govern my church. And these affairs are not to be conducted by manifestations of the Spirit unless these directions and manifestations come through the regularly authorized officers of branch or district. If my people will respect the officers whom I have called and set in the church, I will respect these officers; and if they do not, they can not expect the riches of gifts and the blessings of direction.

5. WCR 705
   Requirement for Baptism
   Adopted April 15, 1913
   705. That all that is required of a candidate requesting baptism is for the candidate to satisfy the church authorities that he is worthy, and that it is not necessary to make a public request.

6. Doctrine and Covenants 17:21
   Baptism is to be administered in the following manner unto all those who repent: The person who is called of God and has authority from Jesus Christ to baptize, shall go down into the water with the person who has presented him or herself for baptism, and shall say, calling him or her by name: Having been commissioned of Jesus Christ, I baptize you in the name of the Father, and of

the Son, and of the Holy Ghost, Amen. Then shall he immerse him or her in the water, and come forth again out of the water.

7. Doctrine and Covenants 17:22d, 23b

    22 d. O God, the eternal Father, we ask thee in the name of thy Son Jesus Christ, to bless and sanctify this bread to the souls of all those who partake of it, that they may eat in remembrance of the body of thy Son, and witness unto thee, O God, the eternal Father, that they are willing to take upon them the name of thy Son, and always remember him and keep his commandments which he has given them, that they may always have his Spirit to be with them. Amen.

    23 b. O God, the eternal Father, we ask thee in the name of thy Son Jesus Christ, to bless and sanctify this wine to the souls of all those who drink of it, that they may do it in remembrance of the blood of thy Son which was shed from them, that they may witness unto thee, O God, the eternal Father, that they do always remember him, that they may have his Spirit to be with them. Amen.

8. Doctrine and Covenants 86:1c

    And behold, this should be wine; yea, pure wine of the grape of the vine, of your own make. And again, strong drinks are not for the belly, but for the washing of your bodies.

9. Doctrine and Covenants 26:1b

    For, behold, I say unto you, that it mattereth not what ye shall eat, or what ye shall drink, when ye partake of the sacrament, if it so be that ye do it with an eye single to my glory;

10. WCR 702

    Sacrament Wine

    Adopted April 9, 1913

    702. That fermented wine should not be used in the Sacrament services of the church, but that either unfermented wine or water should be used, and so be in harmony with the spirit of the revelations.

11. WCR 172

    Bread and Wine Use

    Adopted April 10, 1875

    172. That the bread and wine used at the sacrament are simply blessed for the use of those who at the time, and with an understanding of its purpose, partake of it, in no way relating to its subsequent use; therefore it is unnecessary to pass the bread until all be taken.

12. Doctrine and Covenants 111:2b

    "You both mutually agree to be each other's companion, husband and wife, observing the legal rights belonging to this condition; that is, keeping yourselves wholly for each other, and from all others, during your lives?"

13. WCR 701

    Ordinance of Blessing

    Adopted April 9, 1913

    701. That the ordinance of blessing should not be administered to children who are old enough to be baptized.

Chapter 5

Discipleship, Reconciliation, and Justice Making through the Sacraments

Introduction

In all our discussion about sacraments it is important to remember that Jesus Christ is the first sacrament from which all the sacraments of the church take their meaning. Jesus is God's way revealed in all its fullness. Jesus is the model of what it means to live a full, peaceable-kingdom life. If you want to live a life that speaks of Zion, look at and follow Jesus. Jesus embodies a life of justice to others. Ritual without commitment to justice is false religion, thundered the prophets of old (Amos 5:21-24; Micah 6:6-8). The sacraments, to be true and faithful to the divine intent, must include our commitment to follow Jesus in a just and peacemaking life.

The sacraments are also the international language of the church practiced whenever the Community of Christ is faithful in making disciples of all nations. The sacraments call us into relationship as followers of Jesus and shape us into the body of Christ, an international family of brothers and sisters, that transcends culture, race, and nationality. Our compassionate commitment to others should therefore embrace all humanity.

Each one of our eight sacraments helps guide us more closely into the life of Jesus, his passion for making peace, and living a just life. Sacraments bring together the influence of the Holy Spirit, the example of the life of Jesus, and one's personal commitment of faith in blessing and empowerment. The sacraments point to the presence of God everywhere and that all of life is potentially sacred. The sacraments point to God's yearning love to bring all humans into peace, wholeness, and right relationships with each other and the Divine. This is what the Hebrews meant by the word *shalom*, a richer and fuller word than the English word "peace."

"Peace" in English normally means the absence of conflict or war. This is a lesser or negative peace. The greater or positive peace of shalom includes reconciliation, harmony, just and right relationships with each other in community, health, and salvation. The word Jesus used was shalom.[1]

Likewise the Hebrew word Jesus used for justice, *sedeqah*, and translated in Greek as *dikaiosune*, also means righteousness. Again the Hebrew word *sedeqah*, like shalom, is fuller and richer than the concept of justice commonly understood in English. Justice in the Hebrew sense is more about restoring and healing damaged relationships than punishment. *Sedeqah* in the Old Testament, and *dikaiosune* and related words in the New Testament, are translated into English in a variety of ways. New Testament scholar Chris Marshall argues that the English-language reader of the Bible seldom realizes how central the concept of justice is in both Testaments.[2]

We are blessed in the Community of Christ tradition with the concept of Zion, which is concretely and robustly defined as a people "of one heart and one mind, dwelling in righteousness with no poor among them" (see Doctrine and Covenants 36:2h-i). Living justly, righteously, is central to Zion. Zion is conveyed much more adequately through shalom and *sedeqah* than the English words "peace and justice." Zion has been defined as process, condition, and place. Shalom is the condition. Acting justly and working at reconciliation, as disciples of Jesus, is the process. Place may be congregation, neighborhood, village, city, nation, or the whole world.

We will now look at each sacrament in turn. We will see how each helps shape and form followers of Jesus into full participants in the peaceable kingdom, or Zion.

Baptism – A Covenant with God and Each Other

In conversation with Nicodemus, Jesus told him that he had to be born again of water and spirit to enter the kingdom of God:

> **Jesus answered [Nicodemus], "Very truly, I tell you, no one can see the kingdom of God without being born from above." Nicodemus said to him, "How can anyone be born after having grown old? Can one enter a second time into the mother's womb and be born?" Jesus answered, "Very truly, I tell you, no one can enter the kingdom of God without being born of water and Spirit...." –John 3:3-5 NRSV**

Both baptism of water and confirmation of the Holy Spirit by the laying on of hands seek to be faithful to this teaching in the Gospel of John. Rebirth is a dramatic way of saying humans have to begin all over again if they are to see and enter the kingdom of God. The first time we are born, we are born American, German, Kenyan, Indian, Haitian, or some other nationality. To be born again we leave our tribe or nation to become first of all citizens of the kingdom of God. Our country then is the whole world and every other human being is a fellow citizen because God's kingdom is a nation for others. We are now internationalists, not nationalists.

Baptism requires personal faith in Jesus. It is a response to God's love expressed through Jesus Christ. To follow the discipleship theme, for instance in Matthew's Gospel, we see that baptism is a choice to follow

Jesus' example "to fulfill all righteousness" (Matthew 3:15). Shortly after Jesus' baptism he called the first four disciples (Matthew 4:18-22) and then taught them the Sermon on the Mount (Matthew 5-7).

Those who seek to follow Jesus through the waters of baptism must also know and live the Sermon on the Mount to "fulfill all righteousness." This includes loving our enemies (Matthew 5:43-48), seeking first the kingdom of God and its justice/righteousness (Matthew 6:31-33), choosing the narrow way (Matthew 7:13), and building our lives on the rock of Christ's teachings rather than the sand of this world's ways (Matthew 7:24-27). The Sermon on the Mount is the constitution of the peaceable kingdom, Zion. A disciple following Jesus through baptism is choosing to live according to the ways of Zion. The Gospel of Matthew ends with the Great Commission:

> Go therefore and make disciples of all nations, baptizing them in the name of the Father and of the Son and of the Holy Spirit, and teaching them to obey everything that I have commanded you. —Matthew 28:19-20

Baptism is publicly testifying that you are choosing to follow Jesus with all of your heart, might, mind, and strength. Baptism thus is a decision that marks a significant point in the process of repentance from all that is selfish, violent, and unjust. It is a voluntary step taken because of the joy of committing one's life to Jesus and his vision of the kingdom of God on earth. In our tradition you thus have to be at least eight years old, which is recognized as the age of accountability. It is a step requiring personal and informed decision. No one can decide for us to become a follower of Jesus. Only we as individuals can do that.

We deal with our past by confessing our sins in detail to God and possibly to a trusted person and seek to make full amends where wise and possible. Baptism then also becomes an outer and inner cleansing that begins a new way of life for as long as we live.

We practice baptism by full immersion. The word *baptizo* is Greek for immersion. We are buried with Christ in the water and rise to "walk in newness of life" and symbolically participate in Christ's death and resurrection (see Romans 6:3-4). Every part of the life of a disciple has to be immersed in the gospel, including our wallets. We are committing ourselves to keep the commandments of Jesus, which includes welcoming the stranger, feeding the hungry, loving our enemies, and visiting the sick and the imprisoned. We change from participating in all systems that make for death and humiliation of others to working for life in all its joyful fullness.

To recite clear vows at baptism as we do in the covenant of marriage may be very helpful to make clear the nature of the commitment being made. For example, the following is based on the prayer on the bread at Communion (Doctrine and Covenants 17:22d) and consists of these promises:

Minister:	Are you willing to take upon you the name of Jesus Christ?
Candidate:	I am.
Minister:	Are you willing to always remember Jesus Christ in all that you think, do, and say?
Candidate:	I am.
Minister:	Are you willing to keep the commandments of Jesus now and henceforth?
Candidate:	I am.
Minister:	Then may you have the Spirit of Jesus to always be with you as you take this step of baptism and confirmation.

In a similar way Doctrine and Covenants 17:7a-d, which very beautifully describes the conditions for baptism, could also be adapted as vows.

We enter baptism making a covenant or contract with God and with other baptized brothers and sisters in Christ. Baptism thus has vertical and horizontal dimensions in the covenant. We covenant with God. We covenant with other sisters and brothers. Together we covenant to allow God to work through us so that the peaceable kingdom of God, with the fruits of justice and peace, may become visible and tangible on earth.

Confirmation – Power to Live Justly and for Reconciliation

Jesus began his public ministry according to Luke by reading the following passage from Isaiah 61:1-2/58:6:

> **The Spirit of the Lord God is upon me,**
> **because the Lord has anointed me;**
> **to bring good news to the oppressed,**
> **to bind up the brokenhearted, to proclaim liberty to the capatives**
> **and release to the prisoners.**
> **To proclaim the year of the Lord's favor...**

The Holy Spirit is inseparably connected with justice for the poor in the life of Jesus. We see the same in the first church in Jerusalem. At Pentecost the Holy Spirit comes and the disciples live with all things in common, so poverty is abolished in their fellowship together (see Acts 2).

After baptism the elders pray for the Holy Spirit to do its full work in the newly baptized disciple. This is confirmation—confirmation that the

Holy Spirit will work in the new disciple to live a new life that will join with others in liberating the poor.

We believe the Holy Spirit is the Spirit of Jesus and gives the power to live rightly with God and others. The work of the Holy Spirit in a disciple's life is to bring about "fruit": "love, joy, peace, patience, kindness, generosity, faithfulness, gentleness, and self-control" (Galatians 5:22-23). In our own strength it is not possible to live the Sermon on the Mount or a kingdom life. With the Holy Spirit and the help of the fellow disciples we can.

Communion – Commitment to Living by the Commandments of Jesus

Communion is about three meals and three stories: Passover, the Lord's Supper, and the messianic banquet.

Jesus began the sacrament of Communion, of sharing bread and wine, the night before his crucifixion when he and his disciples celebrated the annual Passover meal together. The Passover meal celebrates the liberation of the Israelite slaves from bondage in Egypt (see Exodus 1-15). God heard the suffering of the enslaved people and called Moses to lead them from captivity to freedom. The Passover meal remains an important and popular Jewish festival. It uses unleavened bread to remind the participants that their ancestors had to leave in a hurry without time to make proper bread. Communion thus has roots in this powerful and central story of justice and God's compassion for the oppressed. We recall the words of God to Moses:

> **I have observed the misery of my people in Egypt; I have heard their cry…indeed I know their sufferings, and I have come down to deliver them….** –Exodus 3:7-8

Jesus used the symbolism of the Passover meal to point to his own sacrifice, which would deliver the poor from oppression. We remember that Jesus was executed because he dramatically protested the economic abuses of the chief priests in the Jerusalem temple, as they cheated the poor by exorbitant charges for devotional sacrifices. This was the final act of all that Jesus had done in advocating for the marginalized, which led the chief priests and scribes to decide to kill him (Mark 11:15-19). At this first Lord's Supper, as Jesus shared bread and wine, he asked them to repeat this occasion in memory of him (Luke 22:19-20). On the road to Emmaus, after the crucifixion of Jesus, the breaking of bread became the sacrament of recognition of the resurrected Christ (Luke 24:13-35). As in

Passover, human cruelty and oppression are remembered in the Lord's Supper with the victory of God over evil.

The final victory over evil is celebrated in the messianic banquet at Jesus' second coming. The messianic banquet is the joyful feast that celebrates the complete victory over evil and the full coming of the kingdom of God on earth. The messianic banquet has its roots throughout Isaiah but especially Isaiah 25:6-8 and is echoed in Matthew (for example: centurion's servant, 8:5-13; Canaanite woman ,15:21-28; the vineyard, 21:33-46; the great supper, 22:1-14; and the parable of the wedding feast, 25:1-13); and in Luke (for example, 14:15-24).[3] This story is still to be fully told and the feast celebrating the full coming of the kingdom is yet to be eaten. However, the return of Jesus and the future healing of the earth with justice and shalom are promised in the Lord's Supper.

The Communion prayer on the bread, offered by a priest or an elder, challenges and calls us to deep and faithful discipleship:

> O God, the eternal Father, we ask thee in the name of thy Son Jesus Christ, to bless and sanctify this bread to the souls of all those who partake of it, that they may eat in remembrance of the body of thy Son, and witness unto thee, O God, the eternal Father, that they are willing to take upon them the name of thy Son, and always remember him and keep his commandments which he has given them, that they may always have his Spirit to be with them. —Doctrine and Covenants 17:22d

Communion is a meal of remembering Jesus. We remember Jesus as a servant who washed the feet of his disciples. We remember Jesus as a healer, teacher, reconciler, and advocate for the poor. We remember that Jesus was crucified by imperial Rome. Communion opens our eyes to see clearly the injustices of government and empire, the rich and the powerful. It is a meal of commitment to keep the commandments of Jesus, many of which refer to doing justice for the poor. This is one reason we have a special offering for the poor at Communion—the oblation offering. Finally there is the glorious promise of the Holy Spirit to continually empower us as we seek to live by the commandments of Jesus.

Yet Communion is also more than remembering. Jesus, after his resurrection, journeyed with two disciples on the road to Emmaus and helped them remember recent events and what the scriptures said. As nightfall neared, Jesus was invited to join them for supper. When Jesus broke bread with them the disciples' "eyes were opened" and they fully met Jesus (see Luke 24:13-35). So it is in the sacrament of Communion. We can go beyond remembering to encounter the Spirit of Jesus in the here and now and in the joy of his presence also have our "eyes opened" to the promise and mission of Jesus.

We leave Communion committed to work for a world with no more crucifixions, no more victims. And so we are invited to work against the death penalty wherever it exists, to work against the forces of violence whether in the family, in the neighborhood, or among nations. We are called through Communion to speak truth to power, to love our enemies, and to work for economic justice for all so that no child anywhere goes to bed hungry or afraid.

Communion is a sacrament for forming genuine, authentic, Christian community. We come together around the Communion table to share its grace so that our eyes are opened to see our own sin and the great and marvelous grace of the peaceable kingdom. It is a meal of three meals and three stories: Passover, the Lord's Supper and the messianic banquet. But there really are other stories and other meals. My story and your story of growing faith are part of the story of Communion, and every meal we eat should, through our generosity, be a meal shared with the hungry and dispossessed. Every meal and all our stories of faith then become sacramental and redemptive.

Ordination – Specialist Ministries of Reconciliation

All ministers are ministers of reconciliation. Each minister, whatever his or her calling, helps the process of reconciliation between God and each person and among people in families and all other relationships. As Paul wrote:

> **So if anyone is in Christ, there is a new creation: everything old has passed away; see, everything has become new! All this is from God, who reconciled us to himself through Christ, and has given us the ministry of reconciliation; that is, in Christ God was reconciling the world to himself, not counting their trespasses against them, and entrusting the message of reconciliation to us.**
> **—II Corinthians 5:17-18 NRSV**

We believe all are called and gifted to serve others. The highest calling is truly to be a disciple. Some are called and after a time of preparation, are ordained to special ministries. We believe that both women and men may be ordained. Most ministers serve without pay from the church. They have other jobs and work unselfishly as ministers through their jobs as well as serving in congregational life.

There are usually four kinds of specialized ministry in a local congregation. The **deacon** is an advocate for the poor and cares for the physical well being of people in their homes as well as in congregational meetings. Deacons are the first to welcome people to the congregation regardless of their past or their race, class, nationality, or culture. The **teacher** is a peacemaker, skilled in reconciliation among the disciples, and works to lead others in right ways of living. The **priest** has a major concern for prayer in families and that all do their duty, living justly with each other. **Elders** share a major responsibility for pastoral care of the congregation as well as being missionaries. This includes a deep concern for the poor. A pastor is usually an elder and is selected each year by the congregation. The work of the pastor is shared among the other elders, priests, teachers, deacons, and members.

Other specialized elders are called to have a wider ministry among a number of congregations and sometimes internationally. Twelve **apostles** are called as special witnesses of Jesus and of the worth of all persons throughout the world. Each coordinates the missionary work of the church in a geographical area. **Seventies** are also missionaries and especial witnesses of Jesus and the worth of all persons. **High priests** are ministers of vision, called to bear the burdens of troubled lives of people and seek reconciliation. **Bishops** are advocates of economic justice for all and are responsible for looking after the finances and properties of the church and the teaching of stewardship. **Evangelists** are spiritual ministers who are free from administrative responsibilities to give a personal ministry of guidance, counseling, and blessing among those seeking to be disciples living the peaceable kingdom life. Finally, the **prophet-president**, assisted by two counselors, leads the church in seeking God's will for its mission and work as it pursues peace, reconciliation, and healing of the spirit worldwide.

The purpose of these different kinds of specialized ministries is twofold. First, it recognizes that God blesses people with different gifts in living the peaceable kingdom life. Second, these ministers are to work together so that the healing, teaching, and peace- and justice-making ministries of Jesus continue in the world for its salvation. Together these different ministers are

> **to equip the saints for the work of ministry, for building up the body of Christ, until all of us come to the unity of the faith and of the knowledge of the Son of God, to maturity, to the measure of the full stature of Christ.**
> **—Ephesians 4:12-13**

Laying On of Hands for the Sick — Healing of Spirit and Body

Healing ministry is available through the prayers of the elders for those who are sick. This is carried out in the New Testament tradition:

Are any among you sick? They should call for the elders of the church and have them pray over them, anointing them with oil in the name of the Lord. The prayer of faith will save the sick, and the Lord will raise them up; and anyone who has committed sin will be forgiven. –James 5:14-15

The sense of peace that comes from the quiet presence of the Holy Spirit is helpful in healing. The Holy Spirit confirms forgiveness and brings healing and reassurance to the sick person and his or her family. The ways of God are truly marvelous and also include the blessings of skilled medical professionals. We remember that health care should be the right of all, especially the poor.

Marriage – A Mutual Partnership for Life

Christian marriage is modeled on the self-giving love between Christ and the church. Marriage is a mutual agreement between two people for life-long companionship. When mutual commitments are made to each other and to God, marriage becomes a covenant between husband and wife as equals. A priest or an elder may conduct a marriage ceremony. As equal partners the man and woman make a life-long commitment to keep themselves wholly for each other and from all others. Through resolving disagreements in a loving manner in a faithful partnership, families, children, and communities are also blessed. The serious and important nature of this covenant requires good preparation before the marriage ceremony. A minister skilled in premarital preparation should be called on to help facilitate this. Marriage preparation normally should begin at least six months before the marriage ceremony.[4] For the continuing flourishing of the relationship, all the commitment of personal discipleship is needed along with continually seeking the Holy Spirit's guidance and power in the relationship. The support of the congregation is also vital.

Blessing of Children – That All Children May Be Blessed

Baby blessing involves the commitment of a supporting community to bless the growing child. While baptism has to be the child's decision when older, parents are invited to make the decision to bring their babies to the elders for a prayer of blessing. The model is Jesus' blessing of young children (see Mark 10:13-16). At this time parents, family, friends, and the congregation covenant to bless the child as he or she grows physically, mentally, emotionally, and spiritually. We also seek to create a world that blesses all children of every race, culture, and nation. A world that is not safe for any child is a fallen, unjust world that we work to redeem.

Evangelist's Blessing – Guidance in the Ways of Discipleship

These are special prayers of blessing, sometimes at times of crisis or key decision making. They are given by an elder called an evangelist. He or she will take time to get to know the person requesting the blessing and with that individual make special prayerful preparation before giving the blessing. The blessing provides counsel and guidance on how individuals, in their unique circumstances, can be disciples, living the ways of the peaceable kingdom. The blessing may be recorded for further reflection and remembrance.

Conclusion

Each of the sacraments is a door into the life of Jesus and his embodiment of shalom and justice. By dramatically using human touch, consecrated oil, water, juice, and a staple food (such as bread) at key times of decision in a person's life, we are connected with each other and God in the invitation of covenant. The sacraments touch us deeply in our human experience in a personal way. At the same time they provide an international language for the church of commitment, discipleship, healing, and mission. The sacraments connect us with Jesus Christ as the primary sacrament. At the same time they enable us, as disciples being formed into the likeness of Jesus, to be a sacramental presence of a loving God in our deeply troubled world.

Discussion Questions

1. Has a sacramental experience brought you a sense of peace with God and others? Briefly share your story. Which sacramental experiences have particularly challenged you to live a new way of life?
2. Read Acts chapter 2 and IV Nephi 1:1-20. These passages were crucial in shaping the early days of the Community of Christ in the 1830s. How does the baptism of repentance and the gift of the Holy Spirit create a new kind of people of God?
3. Read Romans 6:1-4 and John 3:1-8. How does full immersion in baptism dramatically portray choosing a completely new beginning as a follower of Jesus? When a person is reborn, how does that affect his or her nationality?

4. How do stories of Jesus' crucifixion and resurrection and the Passover story of slaves escaping oppression in Exodus (a) enrich our understanding of the meaning of Communion, and (b) call us to a deeper commitment against violence and injustice in our world? How is the oblation offering an important part of Communion in the light of Exodus?

5. Read James 5:13-16. How has the laying on of hands for the sick blessed you or others close to you? What promise of personal peace is resident there?

6. How would you define peace and justice? Is it helpful for you to define peace and justice in terms of Zion, the peaceable kingdom? How is the dream of Zion brought together with commitment to follow Jesus in baptism, Communion, and ordination?

7. Read Ephesians 4:11-13. How is ordination the calling of people with different gifts to work together as a team to help the congregation and the whole church become like Jesus?

8. Read Mark 10:1-12 and Doctrine and Covenants 111:2a-d. How is commitment to justice and reconciliation important in the sacrament of marriage?

9. Read Mark 9:33-37 and 10:13-16, along with III Nephi 8:20-24. Look also at the church seal. How can little children lead us to peace in our families, congregations, and the world?

10. For those who have had an evangelist's blessing, how did that help you? How can preparation for an evangelist's blessing deepen your discipleship and commitment to work for peace and justice in a hurting world?

Notes

1. For the meaning of *shalom* see *Encyclopedia Judaica*, Vol. 13 (New York: Macmillan, 1971): 194-201; and also *The Interpreter's Dictionary of the Bible: An Illustrated Encyclopedia* (Nashville, Tennessee: Abingdon, 1980 [1962]), 704-706. See also Pinchas Lapide *The Sermon on the Mount: Utopia or Program for Action?* (New York: Orbis, 1986), 34-35. An excellent text is P. B. Yoder, *Shalom: The Bible's Word for Salvation, Justice and Peace* (Nappanee, Indiana: Evangel Publishing House, 1987).

2. For *sedeqah* (sometimes spelled *zedakah*) see Christopher D. Marshall, *Beyond Retribution: A New Testament Vision for Justice, Crime and Punishment* (Grand Rapids, Michigan: Eardmans, 2001), chapter 2. See also "Zedakah," *Encyclopedia Judaica*, Vol. 16 (New York: Macmillan, 1971), 961.

3. See Daniel S. Steffen, "The Messianic Banquet and the Eschatology of Matthew," (*www.bible.org/docs/nt/books/mat/banquet.htm*).

4. It is suggested that marriage preparation classes begin at least six months before marriage. This allows a couple time to decide not to get married if this emerges as the right thing. The pressure of commitments made in terms of a reception, invitations sent out, etc., can sometimes trap a couple into marrying unwisely. For the latest information on marriage preparation see *www.CofChrist.org/FamilyMinistries*.

Chapter 6

The Sacraments Are Opportunities for Witness and Sharing

Called to share our witness, the Community of Christ is admonished to relate evangelism and the sacraments. Jesus' emphasis on baptism as a "missionary sacrament"[1] is best captured in the words of the great commission from Matthew 28:19-20: "Go...make disciples of all nations, baptizing them in the name of the Father and of the Son and of the Holy Spirit,...teaching them...." During the early years when Christian fellowship was being shaped into the structure and form of the early church, a strong relationship existed between evangelism and the sacraments of baptism and the Lord's Supper. Today, all eight sacraments of the Community of Christ need to be looked at as missionary sacraments and opportunities for witness and sharing.

Our Doctrine and Covenants calls for greater understanding of the sacraments:

> **Look especially to the sacraments to enrich the spiritual life of the body. Seek for *greater understanding* of my purposes in these sacred rites and prepare to receive a renewed confirmation of the presence of my Spirit in your experiences of worship. —Doctrine and Covenants 158:11c (emphasis added)**

Could not this greater understanding deal with emphasizing them more as opportunities of witness and sharing in outreach to visitors? This chapter will propose ways the eight sacraments of the Community of Christ can be more visitor-friendly instruments of witness and sharing.

An Attitude and an Environment of Hospitality

Most importantly, for all eight sacraments of the Community of Christ to be visitor-friendly instruments of witness and sharing, there must be an attitude and an environment of hospitality. If liturgy is defined as a public work done by worshipers for God, on behalf of others, then by definition liturgy reaches out to all people, proclaiming the "good news" by word and sacrament. And so an attitude and an environment of hospitality are essential to liturgical worship.[2]

Liturgy

All of us are liturgical. This is to say, we all use material and human "forms" to express our worship of God. There simply are no non-liturgical churches. Monastics rising to recite the Night Office, Quakers waiting in silent assurance upon the Spirit, Catholics praying the rosary and revivalists sing hymns of devotion to the name of Jesus, Russian Orthodox ritualists bowing amid incense and icon and Salvation Army evangelists marching to drum and tambourine—all are engaged in liturgy.... As long as we are finite human beings, we must use liturgy; we must express ourselves through forms of worship.

Liturgy—*liturgia*—simply means "the people's work." Our task in liturgy is to glorify God in the various aspects of our worship life. We are to let the reality of God shine through the human or physical forms. This is true whether we are singing hymns or burning candles, dancing in ecstatic praise or bowing in speechless adoration.

—Richard Foster, *Streams of Living Water* (Harper, 1998)

The liturgical worship proclaiming the good news by the sacraments must be open to all with the spirit of hospitality. In the movie *Sister Act*, Whoopi Goldberg plays a nightclub singer in Reno, Nevada, USA named Dolores. After witnessing a murder, Dolores seeks protection from the police. The police want to place her in a convent until it is time for her to testify because she is in grave danger. The monsignor informs the Mother Superior of the convent of Dolores's predicament. Not really excited about having her in the convent, the Mother Superior finally gives in when the monsignor tells her of the large donation the police will give her convent. Upon seeing Dolores in her study with her gold lamé coat, purple-sequined outfit, and a profusion of jewelry, the Mother Superior gasps, quickly leaves, shuts the door, and faces the monsignor. He reminds her in tersely, "You have taken a vow of hospitality to all in need." The Mother Superior replies with a serious, straight face, "I lied."[3]

How many of us in the Community of Christ would say, "I lied when I agreed to take upon myself the name of Jesus Christ as stated in our Communion prayer over the bread"? As exemplified by Christ, we hold as a strong value the worth of all. How many of us would say, "I lied when I agreed to respect the worth of all"?

This respect given to the stranger is vital if we are to reach the visitors in our sacrament services. The word "respect" comes from two Latin roots: *spect,* which means "to watch or to see," and *re,* meaning "again."[4] Thus, when we talk of giving respect to someone, we are "seeing them again" in a new light—the light of Christ. First impressions are not sufficient; it requires an ongoing relationship. And so we must extend hospitality to guests in our midst for an extended period of time if we are to appreciate the true value of visitors and see the presence of the Holy within them.

Those who offer this welcome, this hospitality, to all visitors, often receive far more than they give. Many times those we welcome, however reluctantly, often welcome us in return. Our guests become our hosts and we, as hosts, become the guests. When this happens, God's work within the sacred relationship of hospitality often becomes manifest.[5] For too long we have only thought of ourselves being the hosts to our guests at church. But when we truly tarry with the visitor and truly engage in mutual listening,[6] we establish a relationship of reciprocity, the essence of hospitality. Barbara Howard, Community of Christ minister, points out the Indo-European root of the word "host" is *ghosti*, which is also the root of the word "guest."[7] There is a mutual giving and receiving. To be truly visitor riendly, to truly share our witness, reciprocity must take place.

This is true hospitality. When the congregations of the Community of Christ make this decision for hospitality, we become a link in the chain of hospitality that reaches back through Sarah and Abraham, Jesus and Zacchaeus, and countless disciples throughout the history of our church. Making this decision to extend hospitality to our visitors in the name of Christ, we enter into a sacred relationship where God is present. Matthew 18:20 tells us, "For where two or three are gathered in my name, I am there among them" (NRSV). The Community of Christ, corporately as well as individually, is to be always a giver and a receiver, host and guest, in the services of the sacraments. All of the eight sacraments need to have this element of hospitality.

Elements That Foster Hospitality

Many of our sacraments occur in worship settings open to the wider community. Because the sacraments are special moments in the lives of individuals, friends and family should be encouraged to attend. Special preparation needs to be made by the congregation to welcome guests, to provide information, and to witness of Jesus Christ through the sacraments. Looking at the symbols, music, dress, and inclusive language, and defining unknown words are areas that need to be addressed if our congregations are to extend the hand of hospitality. Hospitality is enhanced when unfamiliar music is rehearsed before each sacrament service. Guests may not feel comfortable dressing up for church, and insufficient income may prevent owning appropriate clothing for some families. Acceptance of all people regardless of their appearance is critical for hospitality. It's also important to provide a clear worship format that is understandable and appropriate for guests.

Sacraments are religious rituals rich with symbols. Physical elements such as bread, water, and oil are used in symbolic ways to point to something beyond themselves. Ritual actions, such as kneeling, placing hands on a person's head, or raising the right hand are also symbolic, with meaning and purpose beyond the mere gestures. Symbols are only effective, however, when they clearly communicate to the participants and observers. When symbols become confusing or meaningless, they cease to function as symbols and become, instead, barriers to understanding. In addition, if the form itself becomes sacrosanct, it defeats the whole purpose of the sacrament: to connect human beings with the Divine. Often, for visitors, seekers, or even members of the Community of Christ, the original intent of our traditional symbols is obscure, and the meaning has been lost in the form. The task for the inviting congregation is to translate and transform the symbols of our sacraments for those who are new to the experience or who have forgotten the symbolic meaning.

In your planning and preparation, consider the following suggestions:

- Be sure your church is "user friendly." Install directional signs to help people find the church building, the parking lot, sanctuary, classrooms, restrooms, and fellowship hall. Assign people to welcome and escort visitors, introduce members, assist with nursery care, and provide for special needs. Prepare a visiting program to make contact with guests after they have visited your church.
- Plan the service with the sacrament central to all that occurs
- Consider the needs of visitors and do the following:
  - Be sure the music chosen is appropriate, easy to sing, and words are available for all to see and follow. Follow copyright regulations.
  - Find out if family members or special guests have musical talents they would be willing to share in the worship.
  - Simplify ritual as much as possible. Keep movements natural and understandable. Consider using family members or special guests to assist in the ritual in appropriate ways. Be sure they understand and have practiced their part.
  - Guide participants through the worship with clear directions. Identify compassionately with people's fears, and encourage participation while giving official sanction to remain an observer.
- For those unfamiliar with our sacraments and traditions, consider printing clarifications in the bulletin, or in a bulletin insert, so that the flow of the service is not interrupted by verbal ex-

planations. Briefly explain any special terminology used, ritual movements, and symbolism of the sacrament. For example, at an ordination service the bulletin insert could include a list of priesthood offices, with simple definitions of words like "Aaronic" and "Melchisedec." In all sacraments, the use of inclusive language and definitions for words unfamiliar to visitors are important elements in hospitality. "Graceland," "Zion," "the Three Standard Books," "reunion," or "D. and C." need explanations or substitutions to convey meaning to newcomers. If our sacraments are to witness to the community, they must open doors of hospitality, not build walls of exclusiveness.

- Free family members who are involved with the sacrament from critical responsibilities so they are available to welcome and greet guests and neighbors.
- Arrange for companions to sit with visitors to help people unfamiliar with the songbooks, or order of the service, without being intrusive on their experience of worship. Be available after the service if the visitor has any questions.

When a sacrament centers on an individual, such as a baptism or ordination, that person functions as a special witness of Christ. The presider should check with the person to see that each symbolic element and act is clear and understandable.

The presider may provide a time when the person can share her or his witness of Jesus and tell a personal experience as it relates to the preparation, performance, and challenge of the sacrament. In addition, during the course of the worship service, remind people of their past experiences with the sacrament. Invite guests to participate fully. Keep the witness of Christ central to the sacrament.

Evaluation following a sacrament can provide valuable information for improvement. Ask the candidate and other church members to evaluate the experience and make suggestions. Check to make sure the symbols and rituals used were understandable and in keeping with our faith traditions. Be willing to hear critique and make adjustments. Be sensitive to the long-standing traditions and the feelings of members who hold dear each element of a sacred ritual, and be open to their critique and suggestions. The intent is not to throw out all tradition but to honor traditional symbols and make them transparent to the uninitiated.

After the worship, engage the visitors in fellowship and be sure to help them with any questions they may have. Learn from each other. Use their fresh perspectives and new eyes to see what we take for granted or comfortably repeat without paying attention to deeper meanings.

Making Sacraments Invitational

Karen Waring, a church member from the British Isles, has discovered the power of the sacraments as an invitational tool to those not yet fully integrated into the Community of Christ. She writes,

> The sacraments provide a good focus for "invitation" or "way in" to home visiting. Since most of the sacraments provide a ministry for those in need—either celebrating a blessing or addressing an anxiety—they intersect with the current life focus in the lives of people. As we visit friends of the church to express our concern or share in their celebration, the gift of the sacraments is a tangible ministry we can offer.
>
> For instance, a teen who attends our youth group recently celebrated the birth of a new sibling in the family. I went to their house to share in their joy. It was a pleasure to talk about God's gift of a child and I was able to involve them more completely in the life of the church by offering the sacrament of infant blessing. The experience of this new birth became an opportunity for them to share with Jesus through the church.
>
> Similarly, when visiting the sick or bereaved, the availability of the laying on of hands can provide an opportunity to become more involved in the life and fellowship of the church. The church has become too "precious" about the sacraments, using them only within the confines of the member-ship. For me the change in understanding occurred when we became free to offer Communion to all. I began to realize the potential for sharing all the sacraments we have.

Making Our Eight Sacraments Visitor Friendly

In addition to these general guidelines, consider each sacrament in its unique beauty as it translates divine purpose into human forms. The following specific suggestions may help visitors and friends relate more fully to each of the sacraments in our faith tradition.

Reaching Out with Baptismal Services

The sacrament of baptism provides an excellent opportunity for witness, challenge, and reaching out to seekers. Going into the water is a personal decision that expresses a promise made to God, a personal relationship with Jesus Christ, and the first step of discipleship. This new beginning is available to everyone of age (eight years or older), with the congregation willing to follow up such beginnings with classes to deepen discipleship and understanding. Keep in mind, however, that the baptismal service itself can provide teaching moments that reach visitors and seekers.

For example, explore the meaning of water, as you move among the congregation with a bowl of clear water. For an experiential emphasis, flick droplets on the congregants as you talk and move. If indoors, invite children and adults to come forward and see the font while baptism is explained. The words of the baptismal formula during the service provide an opportunity to share some of the basics of our belief and identity:

"Jane Brown…"	This is a personal decision; God knows you by name
"…having been commissioned"	Called to servant ministry and given a task
"…by Jesus Christ…"	Christ is central to our faith
"…I baptize you…"	Involved in transformation of old into new
"…in the name of the Father, Son, and Holy Ghost, Amen."	Belief in the Trinity and trust in God

For a visual aid, immerse a cloth in water to demonstrate how light (God) shines through the wet cloth better than a dry one. Mention the support provided by a welcoming member who receives the newly baptized disciple with a clean dry towel. Invite the congregation to stand and welcome the new disciple into the church community with hugs and handshakes. Invite the congregation to remember their own promises to God, made in baptism, in prayer, in times of crisis or blessing. Ask the oldest member to come to the font or river and share her or his testimony of being baptized. This person represents the congregation's closest link to the church of Jesus' day and reminds us of the rich heritage present in the ritual of baptism.

Confirmation and the Newcomer

Confirmation, like blessings and the prayer for healing, uses hands as symbols of service, transmission of authority, the touch of God's Spirit, and connectedness. Touch is an important element in this sacrament. You could invite the people in the pews to hold hands during the confirmation prayer.

Invite congregants to study their own hands and identify ways their hands witness of their daily activities (callouses, nails, scars, dexterity). Is this witness all it could be, or is God's call challenging each one to greater service with those hands? Ask people to hold their hands high, palms up as a symbol of receiving from God. Then ask them to turn their hands over to pour out God's blessings on others. Talk about prayer as blessing, as connection with the Divine, and as communication for living.

Most importantly, confirmation involves inviting more of the Holy Spirit to be present in an individual's life to empower them in their discipleship. Help the congregation understand this by suggesting comparisons such as: electricity for a light bulb, steam for an engine, gasoline for a car, or radio waves for a song.

Because confirmation also means officially becoming a member in the Community of Christ, prepare a tangible way to express the entry into the fellowship, the support and love of the community, and the congregation's promise of guidance and spiritual nurture. Invite congregants to stand when the candidate stands and silently renew their promise of discipleship. As part of the worship, ask the congregants to write a brief statement of welcome, collect them, and give them to the candidate. Pass the Peace among the congregation. Explain that the community is touched by the influence of a new member. Together the candidate and the community go forward into the future with God.

The Lord's Supper as an Evangelistic Experience

The sacrament of the Lord's Supper is designed for people who have already made a commitment to Jesus Christ through the waters of baptism, regardless of their religious tradition, and are familiar with the meaning of the symbols involved. For that very reason, we often assume the symbolic meaning is understood and needs no explanation. Even longtime members of the Community of Christ, however, may need reminders and aids to help them deepen their understanding and commitment. Careful planning with the visitor in mind can transform this sacrament into an evangelistic experience to inform seekers not only about the sacrament itself but also about the beliefs and practices of the Community of Christ.

The Lord's Supper is basically patterned on a meal. Like a real feast, ritual movements include laying the table, preparing food, serving and eating, and cleaning up. Those who serve in leadership positions are often the only members of the congregation who have the opportunity to see, understand, and recognize the ritual movements that occur at the table each Communion Sunday. Some Sunday invite the congregation to come forward and circle the table, while the emblems and table are prepared. The white cloths represent purity and God's sheltering presence. The bread represents life, nourishment, and Jesus as the Bread of Life. The wine symbolizes blood, the essence of Christ's actions and life, the unfermented fruit of discipleship, and sacrificial offering, as well as atonement. Note that this is the only sacrament that uses an altar, a traditional symbol for sacrifice as well as a table for feasting.

There is powerful symbolism of breaking the bread as a way to communicate God's grace, forgiveness, and the worth of persons. God uses broken things: the broken bread and crushed grape, the broken vial of oil, the broken seal of the tomb. God can use the brokenness of humanity to extend grace and to bring about blessings. Kneeling conveys humility before God, reverence, and repentance. Other symbolic actions we use in worship include bowed heads, folded hands, rising to our feet, and closed eyes. Each says something about how we view our relationship to God and God's grace in our lives.

For visitors, prepare a bulletin insert that is a personal invitation from God to share in "table fellowship." This could include on the back or inside a brief description of the ritual, the meaning of the symbols, and definitions of the terms used. Share the inclusiveness of Christ's table fellowship and the customs of hospitality in Jesus' day. Even those who don't participate in Communion can take this time to reflect on their faith journey and do business with Christ. This will assist newcomers in feeling welcome at a sacrament that has been traditionally designed primarily for members. It will also open the door for further exploration into the Community of Christ.

The Ordination Service and Sharing Hospitality

Usually when people attend a celebration, there is a designated host or hostess who takes care of the needs and comfort of the people. In the Community of Christ, the priesthood are charged with providing for the needs of the people and sharing the hospitality of the Holy Spirit with all. Preparation for an ordination service must provide for the needs of many people: the ordinand, the members, family, and visitors, who may be unfamiliar with our terminology and priesthood structure. Your service will be much more meaningful to everyone if you include specific activities that demonstrate the meaning of priesthood and help visitors feel informed at the service.

Many visitors may be unaware of our use of lay ministry in the congregation. Sometimes the talk before the sacrament can briefly allude to the way priesthood responsibilities are shared among many unpaid members of the congregation and would assist visitors in understanding priesthood calls and responsibilities.

Invite ordained priesthood who hold the office of the priesthood candidate to rise and escort the new ordinand to the waiting chair. Ask each to offer a one-sentence statement of the purpose of their ministry or a one-sentence challenge to the ordinand. Prepare a tool kit for the priesthood member, filled with symbols of the calling. Explain to the congregation what is in the tool kit and its significance to the call. A tool kit for an Aaronic teacher could include the following:

- A small cloth—to wipe away tears and restore hope in Jesus Christ
- A towel—to symbolize servant ministry
- A small dove pin—to represent the ministry of peace and reconciliation
- A small candle—to represent watching over the congregation
- A wire fish or fish hook (not real)—to symbolize the call to discipleship

Adapt the kit to other offices by including different elements: a vial of oil for a new elder, a prayer card or prayer mat for a priest, a coin for a deacon, a small fish net for a seventy, a cross for a high priest. Use your imagination, and adapt the kit to the individual as well as to the office.

My Neighbor and the Laying On of Hands for the Sick—Healing of Spirit and Body

The sacrament of laying on of hands for the sick is usually a private ritual, often done in homes, hospitals, or the pastor's study. Most often, the person requesting the sacrament is a member of the church, well aware of the symbolism involved. It does not need to be limited to members, however, and by making our neighbors and friends aware of the meaning and importance of this sacrament, the laying on of hands can be a valuable tool for introducing people to the church. When members know that a neighbor or friend is suffering illness of body or spirit, they can visit the sick and mention that our church performs this sacrament.

In explaining the sacrament to neighbors, however, the emphasis should not be placed on guarantees of physical healing. The intent of "administration" or laying on of hands is to place the candidate in God's loving arms for whatever blessing God may grant. "Curing" must often take second place to a greater "wholeness" in terms of relationships, both with the Divine and with others.

At times, it is appropriate to offer the sacrament of laying on of hands as part of a larger worship experience. When this is done, the presider should clearly explain the procedure for the sake of any visitors present. The oil is a continuation of the ancient tradition of anointing the head of kings with oil to symbolize the favor of God. The oil also has represented the "balm for healing." In the laying on of hands, oil symbolizes the outpouring of God's love toward the individual, and God's ever-present desire to bless and make whole. It is important to stress that the oil itself has no healing properties, but only symbolizes the love of God. In public worship, as in sharing with a neighbor, the intent is for wholeness of spirit and relationships, regardless of God's will in terms of physical healing. We pray to the God of the Cross, who knows what it means to suffer pain and death, who understands physical distress, and who weeps with us in our brokenness. We place our loved ones in the compassionate and understanding arms of this God who understands both crucifixion and resurrection, for we know that the divine promise to be present will never fail. When we visit a neighbor who is ill, this is the God who walks with us and will be with the neighbor even through the valley of the shadow of death. How, then, can we possibly withhold from our neighbor our testimony of the loving grace and comfort available to them by knowing our God of the Cross?

Weddings and Guests

In Jesus' day, weddings were not religious ceremonies, nor were they seen as covenants with God. They were purely secular celebrations. Later traditions began adding the concept of receiving a religious blessing as part of the ceremony. In today's world, a religious element is not required for legal matrimony; a civil agreement is sufficient for secular law.

Our faith tradition, however, upholds marriage as a covenant involving not only the two individuals being married, but also God as a partner in the marriage. Weddings performed by Community of Christ ministers, therefore, are good opportunities to inform the many visitors and friends present about some of the beliefs of our church as they pertain to marriage. An example of this would be the special words prescribed for our marriage covenant. The following is adapted from *The Priesthood Manual* (2004 Edition, pp. 218-221) and could serve as the basis for the wedding homily:

> Marriage is a covenant made between two individuals in the presence of God and with the church as witness. The words, "[Do] you both mutually agree to be each other's companion..." (D. and C. 111:2b), indicate the nature of the marriage covenant. You will make a commitment of mutual support, shared responsibility, and love toward each other. The marriage covenant has as its ideal the depth and integrity that characterize God's covenant relationship with humanity. The sacramental nature of the marriage covenant derives from its relationship to God's covenant with humankind. Furthermore, in marriage two individuals embark on a covenant relationship in which they commit themselves to express their best understanding of Christian discipleship.
>
> The marriage relationship is unique. Part of the marriage vow reads as follows: "Keeping yourselves wholly for each other, and from

78

all others, during your lives" (D. and C. 111:2b; see also 42:7d). This statement suggests that spouses enjoy a depth of relationship with and commitment to each other that surpasses that in their relationships with other individuals.... It suggests that spouses hold each other's interests and welfare uppermost when they make decisions regarding the use of their time, money, and other resources.

Marriage is a sacred covenant between husband and wife in which God participates with sanction, blessing, and guidance.... Marriage is sacred when it expresses the nature of God through the relationship of husband and wife. The marriage ceremony, when performed by the authority of the church, is intended to be a solemnization and public witness of the covenanting couple with God, and is thus considered a sacrament. However, the church recognizes that authorized ceremonies, whether in the church or by other authorities, do not guarantee the development of a sacramental relationship.... The key to the success of the covenant that you will make today is love and we need to be reminded that God is love. As you allow God's Spirit of love to become a part of the new home you are creating, your own special, unique love will blossom and grow. Affirm each other's worth as you develop in experience and understanding. Remember and value the best of times; support and strengthen one another through the difficult times. Help one another realize your own unique potential and special giftedness in this new and very special covenant relationship. Today, it begins.

Additional elements may be added to the wedding service that celebrate the heritage of the couple within the Community of Christ. A member from each of the two primary families could be asked to prepare and share a brief statement of the family's religious heritage. The couple may wish to revive the old custom of signing a family Bible (as well as the marriage certificate) as part of the worship experience. One possible symbol of covenant used in some wedding traditions is to tie a white scarf or ribbon around the clasped hands of the bridal couple after the exchange of rings. Many couples use the ritual of the unity candle to symbolize their joined lives. That symbol can be extended to include the covenant with God if the parties light their individual candle from a Christ candle before joining the flames in a unity candle. Or they may wish to arrange two bowls of sand from their ancestral homes, which are poured together and anointed with oil, symbolic of God's outpouring love blessing the union.

Cultural customs and symbols may enhance the marriage ceremony. The Russian and Ukrainian traditions include an embroidered cloth called a *rushnik*, upon which the bridal couple stand. The *arras* or *laso* is often used symbolically in Hispanic weddings. In some cultures the parents of the bride and groom are expected to stand and offer public prayer of blessing and petition for their son or daughter as they enter into marriage. In other cultures, a congregational gift is given the young couple as part of the ceremony. When some will be present who are unfamiliar with the customs or symbols used, explanation can be provided in the service bulletin.

In addition, a simple step often overlooked is to print the name, address, and contact information for the officiating minister in the order of worship, so others may contact her or him if they have questions or wish to find out more about the church. Karen Waring suggests that a wall display of general wedding photos, key beliefs of our church, and contact information for a wedding be posted. She shares further suggestions from her home country:

> In the British Isles couples have to pay for churches, for an organist, and sometimes for a deacon/verger. In the Community of Christ we make no charge so we advertise that we are free! It has become increasingly common for couples to attend premarital discussions with the minister. In this country, these vary from a brief meeting before the ceremony to several weeks or even weekend courses for the couple.[8]

Premarital counseling is strongly advised by our faith tradition, and can not only meet the growing need among couples, but also provide an opportunity to explore spiritual journeys and extend an invitation to those who wish to find a church home to nurture and support their marriage relationship.

The Blessing of Children as a Witnessing Sacrament

The sacrament of baby blessing is one of the most tender and hopeful moments in a young family's life as they begin the adventure of parenthood. While the blessing is for the baby and its future, the worship service surrounding it should be geared to the needs of the parents and family who attend. For this reason, it's important to check with the parents to identify the best time during the service to schedule the prayer of baby blessing. If the mother needs to feed the baby just before the blessing, be sure to arrange the elements of worship so she can participate in important portions of the service, yet also be free to go to another room and feed at the appropriate time. In some cases, the prayer of blessing may need to be scheduled early in the service, with comments and challenge about the sacrament scheduled for afterward. Be flexible in your planning.

This is one of the sacraments that will automatically draw nonmember friends and family into the congregation, so make the most of the opportunity to help visitors understand the sacrament and the church. Invite family and friends to gather around the parents and baby before the blessing, while the congregants hold hands during the blessing prayer. Or invite all members of the child's family to stand and be recognized as a vital part of the baby's heritage and support group. Ask the parents to introduce family members and state their relationship to the child. (Use caution with this suggestion, however, because some people are embarrassed by such public introductions.)

Baby blessings enjoy a long biblical heritage, including the Jewish tradition of mother and baby going to the temple eight days after birth, to present a sacrifice of purification before God. When Mary brought Jesus to the temple for this rite, Simeon and Anna both spontaneously blessed the infant Jesus. You could ask the congregation members to offer their own spontaneous blessings and wishes for the child, either verbally or written on paper, to be included in the baby's scrapbook. An alternative activity is to invite congregants to remain seated and stretch their hands toward the baby and parents. In this attitude of support provide a moment of silence while the participants offer a silent prayer of support and love for the young family.

Mark records that as an adult, Jesus took the children up in his arms and blessed them. As a special children's moment in the service, invite all the children and youth under the age of eighteen who have been blessed to come forward. If the children are not sure, they can ask their parents. Give each a small card or bookmark of Jesus blessing the children as a remembrance of their blessing.

Be sure that visitors know that the sacrament of baby blessing is open to all babies, regardless of the religious affiliation of their parents. Karen Waring has found that an informational wall chart posted in the foyer or fellowship hall can be effective in extending an invitation to visitors to bring an infant for the sacrament of blessing:

> The display contains photographs of blessings, sample invitations and celebration cards, the main points of our belief, a contact number for more information, and an invitation to participate in the sacrament. At the very least, the display prompts discussion within the groups that use the building. At its best, it means we can offer the gospel in a tangible form to others. In addition, I ran a preschool in the 1990s, which provided me a natural arena for sharing with nonchurch mothers the concept of infant blessing. The potential for outreach exists wherever parents and babies gather for mutual support and encouragement.

The Evangelist's Blessing Reaches My Friend

Evangelist's blessings are not just for members of the Community of Christ. Many people can testify to the witness and spiritual outreach provided when a neighbor or friend is given the opportunity to prepare for and receive an evangelist's blessing. Edith Gallagher of Yorktown, Virginia, USA is only one voice among many who affirm the efficacy of making this sacrament available to friends:

> I have a friend from college that I have known for more than thirty-five years. She was for many years completely unchurched, but about six years ago she was baptized and confirmed in the Catholic Church. I was very supportive of that for her and we spent many hours sharing our churches with each other. I shared with her about the evangelist's blessing and sent her one of the brochures about it. I told her the blessing was for anyone who sought it out and prepared for it. She decided after some study and prayer that she would very much like to have a blessing. She eventually flew from Atlanta to Independence and met with Velma Ruch, who worked with her and gave her a blessing. She feels it was and is a very valuable piece of her spiritual journey. I think it is important the blessing be offered in this way and made available. What an incredible experience and way to share God's love!

Edith continues:

> The transition time between high school and career or college is a difficult time and one in which blessing and assurance is a real need. I feel our young adults at least need to be informed and knowledgeable about the avenue of blessing available to them. Last year at senior high camp I taught the senior high class. More than half of our campers were not Community of Christ members, but one day I spent the entire time talking about God's desire to bless each of us individually as well as a community. I shared with them the sacrament of the evangelist's blessing as one way to receive that blessing. I gave them the brochures and let them ask questions and discuss the possibilities. Most of the counselors had not had blessings either but several showed interest afterward.

> Even from the pulpit the evangelist's blessing can be held up. God *is* a God of blessing and desires very much to show us his love. If we find ourselves preaching particularly about life's difficulties and God's greatest desire for us, or if we are speaking and preaching about the sacraments as a whole, we can mention the evangelist's blessing as one avenue to receive that love and blessing in a very special and unique way. I understand this is not a sacrament that is celebrated or practiced in a public forum. However, I believe that is all the more reason it should be talked about and shared with member and friend alike. Why would we want to hide something so potentially wonderful, transforming, healing, and affirming? Let's talk about it more, not less; more deeply, not just in passing, and let all know [of] God's willingness to use this sacramental process to express divine love and concern.

Here in Edith's heartfelt witness is a glimpse of the transforming nature of our sacraments and the way they can be used to reach seekers, newcomers, and the unchurched. We who have often participated in the sacraments tend to take them for granted, and we forget the power of new life and new possibilities resident in their symbols. These sacraments represent possibilities worth sharing with those we care about. Symbols newly discovered can resonate with the grace and love of God drawing close to individuals through ritual and tradition. Our task—our challenge—is to be the voice of introduction and invitation to all. Come and see. Come and share. Come and be touched by the Divine. In our sacraments, the Holy reaches the human through word and action. God *is* with us! Who would not share such good news with others?

Community Building/Reconciling Dimensions of Sacraments

We celebrate many of the sacraments as a corporate body: the Lord's Supper, baptism, confirmation, ordination, baby blessing, marriage, even the laying on of hands in rare instances. Each of these occasions can be opportunities for the ministry of reconciliation to occur, as the body draws together in worship to deepen the relationship with the Divine.

The Lord's Supper, also called Communion, is obviously a time of reconciliation and community building, as congregants individually remember their covenant relationship to God and their commitment to one another. The Lord's Supper recalls Matthew 5:23-24: "So when you are offering your gift at the altar, if you remember that your brother or sister has something against you, leave your gift there before the altar and go; first be reconciled to your brother or sister, and then come and offer your gift." The intent of Communion is to be reconciled one with another, as well as draw close to God. The days are past when priesthood self-righteously refused to serve bread and wine to a member in conflict with another, but the need for each person to examine his or her relationships is still valid. If the scriptures teach us anything, it is that God cares how we treat one another. The Ten Commandments, the Great Commandment, the Law of Love, and the teachings of Jesus teach us that loving, reconciled relationships are at the heart of the gospel message.

Thus, baptism requires repentance and a new beginning—not just internally but also in terms of the way one treats family, friends, and strangers. Confirmation is entry into the community—an expansion of the reconciling body of Christ to include a new person. Ordination requires personal sacrifice and reconciliation to God's will through serving others—a commitment that builds community and actively involves ordinands in reconciling ministry, regardless of the office. Baby blessings and evangelist's blessings both assist individuals in deepening their relationship with God and becoming better disciples; but they also impact families through the support and encouragement of the body, the commitment of the individual to new disciplines, and the spiritual interactions with others in the course of preparation for the sacraments. Finally, the laying on of hands can be clearly identified as a ministry of reconciliation. We place the person who is ill—be it physically, emotionally, mentally, or spiritually—in the loving arms of God and pray for wholeness, both in the relationship with God and with others.

The movie *Places in the Heart* concludes with a vivid depiction of the reconciling nature of the sacraments in the lives of broken people. The story centers around the accidental homicide of a white police officer by a black youth in the 1930s in the United States, when racial segregation was the norm in the South. The movie explores deep feelings surrounding the lynching of the youth by an angry mob and the various relationships affected in that community.

In the concluding scene, the local minister leads the congregation in the sacrament of Communion. As the bread is passed from congregant to congregant, the movie audience recognizes key individuals who have been involved in greed, infidelity, brutality, duplicity, and racism—conflicts that have divided the townspeople and forever transformed lives. Participating in this unifying, reconciling act are those portrayed as most compassionate in the community, alongside those who are depicted as most bigoted and greedy. The bread and cup are passed to the dead police officer, who turns with a small smile and hands it on to the black youth who shot him. They sit side by side in the congregation, both victims of the brokenness of the society in which they lived, both reconciled to one another and to God in that act of Communion. God's reconciling love is larger than life, wider than reality—it embraces all people, all sinners, all victims, with an invitation to come home and be reconciled.

The symbolism extends beyond a poignant closing to a powerful movie. It speaks to us of the grace of God, which underlies all our symbolic rituals and unites us in a love beyond all human understanding. One of our presiders who has integrated this truth into his own life clearly states the invitation to reconciling communion each Sunday when he welcomes the people. "We are people of the table," he tells his congregation. "Everyone is invited, because God defines the table." The congregation always has a table at the front of their sanctuary to symbolize this truth, and being "people of the table" defines who this congregation is. Table hospitality has become central to their identity and their mission as a congregation and extends to their homes as they invite others.

The sacraments are given for the benefit of the body of Christ in all its human diversity and complexity. As you continue to experience the wholeness and new life offered through the Community of Christ sacraments, you are called and challenged to look for ways to share these opportunities with others, to bring them closer to Christ and enable their spiritual journey of discipleship, reconciliation, and service.

Questions

1. Define "missionary sacrament" in your own terms. Apply the concept to one of the eight Community of Christ sacraments besides baptism.

2. The text talks about the reciprocal hospitality between members of the church and guests. Explain what that means and give an example from your own experience.

3. Review the practical suggestions listed under the subhead "Elements That Foster Hospitality." Identify the suggestions your congregation already implements. Identify two more suggestions you can begin implementing to make your congregation more hospitable.

4. Choose one of the eight sacraments in the subhead "Making Our Sacraments Visitor Friendly." Evaluate each of the suggestions presented for that specific sacrament, in terms of its practical implementation in your congregation. Explain why each suggestion could or could not be implemented. Brainstorm some additional ideas for making the sacrament more understandable and symbolic for a guest visiting for the first time. Be prepared to share your evaluation and brainstorming with the class.

5. When have you participated in a sacrament that had special meaning for you? What made it special? How can you reproduce that experience for others?

6. Imagine yourself explaining the Community of Christ baptismal statement to a nonmember. How does it reflect who we are as a denomination? What words would you use to communicate to someone with no knowledge of our church?

7. Reread the explanation about preparing a "ministry kit" to present to a newly ordained priesthood member. What elements would go into a "ministry kit" for an elder? for a deacon? for a priest?

8. How would you explain our sacrament of evangelist's blessing to a nonmember? Role play telling a friend about this sacrament and inviting the individual to consider participating in this sacrament.

9. When have you seen the ministry of reconciliation offered through the celebration of a sacrament? Share the experience with others.

Notes

1. Mons A. Teig, "Baptism, Evangelism, and Being Church," *Word and World* 14, no. 1:28-35.

2. Sally Morgenthaler, *Worship Evangelism* (Grand Rapids, Michigan: Zondervan, 1995), 262.

3. Elizabeth Rankin Geitz, *Entertaining Angels: Hospitality Programs for the Caring Church* (Harrisburg, Pennsylvania: Morehouse Publishing, 1993), 22.

4. Luther E. Smith Jr., *Intimacy and Mission: Intentional Community as Crucible for Radical Discipleship* (Scottsdale, Pennsylvania: Herald Press, 1994), 164.

5. Geitz, 28.

6. Ibid., 29.

7. Barbara Howard, "Faithful Discipleship," *Saints Herald* 138, no. 11 (November 1991): 15.

8. Editor's note: It may be appropriate for congregations to charge a nominal rental fee for use of their building by those who are not members of their congregation, as well as cleanup and security/damage deposits.

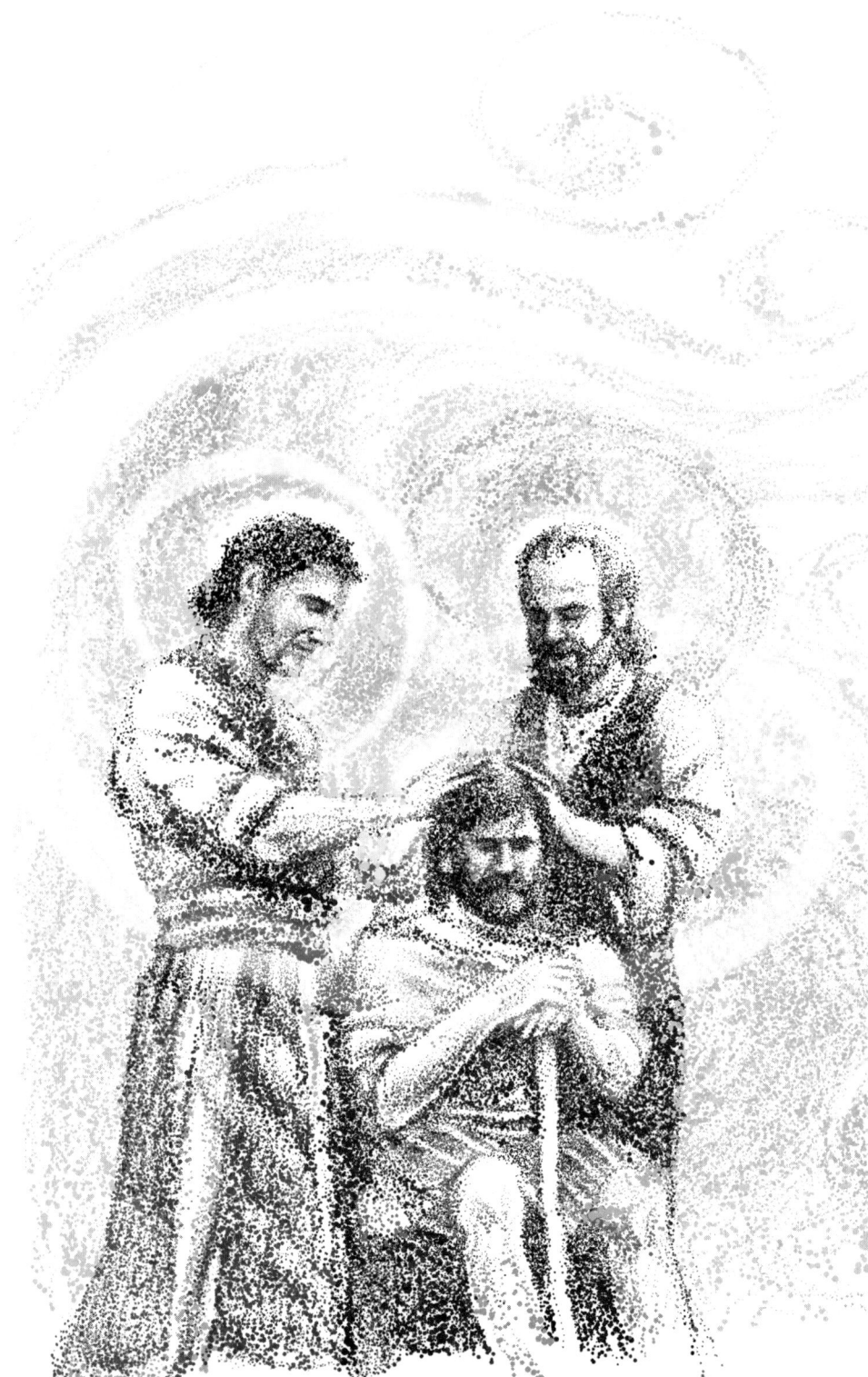

Chapter 7

Sample Services

Six sacraments of the church—baptism, confirmation, ordination, baby blessing, marriage, and Communion—are usually celebrated in public worship. Such celebrations deserve to be thoughtfully planned and practiced in such a way that God is honored and the worshiping community is blessed. Worship is the work of God's people. All are called to take an active part.

Brad Bergland, in his book *Reinventing Sunday*, offers the following observations:

1. Worship is offered to God as worship, and not primarily Christian education or even evangelism.
2. Worship is what the worshipers do for God *and allow God to do to us.*
3. Worship leadership is not performance, although many of the skills are the same.
4. Worship can transform our lives and relationships. It allows us to become more trusting and faithful.
5. Worship expands our souls, makes us generous, and sends us into the world to love and to serve.
6. Worship is a journey into the unknown toward God. It has flow and movement.

Skillful planning and good worship leadership do not have to be sophisticated, complex, or flawlessly executed. Congregational worship is a volunteer endeavor where the gifts of all are honored. Even so, worship involving sacramental ritual should be neither haphazard nor careless. Those who are given leadership responsibilities are rightly expected to plan ahead, to attend to details, and to make spiritual preparation for the experience. Worship planning for a sacramental service should begin several weeks before the date.

When possible, the entire focus of the worship service should be on the sacrament. If more than one sacrament is celebrated, the service should be planned in sections so that attention is given to each sacrament individually.

The following suggestions are offered to remind and assist the worship planner and leader in his or her role.

1. Plan ahead!
2. Identify the focus of the service. Use both a theme and foundational

scripture for the worship experience. Use the lectionary-suggested scripture and Community of Christ suggested theme when possible.

3. Select the elements of worship to be included in the service. Keep the flow of the service simple. Generally, use elements familiar to the worshiping community. Originality and surprise are not the same thing. Give special attention to how the elements of worship flow from one to another. Don't be afraid to schedule silent moments during the service.

4. Be sensitive to the season of the year and the Christian calendar. An Advent Communion service is different from a Pentecost Communion service.

5. Integrate a variety of styles into the service, especially in the music, choosing elements and texts that illuminate the sacrament and theme.

6. Be sensitive to time and pace. Sacrament services do not need to be longer than regular worship services.

7. Choose the people who will provide leadership of the different elements during the service. Worship participants and officiants should be selected according to their giftedness.

8. The presider needs to have a total familiarity with the service and be prepared to deal with any eventuality.

9. Determine who will officiate or perform the sacrament. In some cases, it is appropriate to involve the candidates in this decision (baptism, confirmation, baby blessing, etc.).

10. Be sensitive to the different age groups and interests within the congregation.

11. Plan for a sermon. Ensure that the preacher uses scripture as the foundation of his or her remarks. Limit the speaker to fifteen minutes or less, focused on the sacrament.

12. Communicate in advance with every participant.

13. Make certain those providing music ministry have been given sufficient notice and time to rehearse.

14. Make sure worship participants, especially readers, practice their parts before the service.

15. Prepare a printed bulletin, if desired. In many congregations, these orders of worship serve as a "keepsake" of the sacramental ritual.

16. Unfamiliar music to be sung by the congregation should be rehearsed before the service.

17. Make the worship setting visually compelling—a feast for the eyes! Ensure that the worship space is clean, inviting, and prepared to accommodate the worshipers.

18. Inform the head usher of the logistics of the service, particularly those involving the sacramental ritual and the offering.

Sample Sacrament Worship Services

The following are samples of worship services that include the celebration of a sacrament. These sample services are designed for use by those who live in developed nations and within a Western cultural setting. They will have varying applicability in other contexts. In addition, these service outlines are meant as beginning suggestions for worship planners and need to be tailored to individual congregational circumstances. Each worship service is presented in an annotated format, with numbers inserted in the order of worship corresponding to planning notes, details, and suggestions for the worship planner found at the end of each service outline.

These and other sacrament service suggestions are available on the church's Web site: *www.CofChrist.org/worship*.

The sample sacrament services are in the following order, with the addition of a funeral service:

Baptism

Confirmation

Communion

Ordination

Laying On of Hands for the Sick

Marriage

Blessing of Children

Congregational Blessing

Memorial and Graveside Service

Come to the Water
A Sacramental Covenant
of Baptism

[2]Gathering and Preparation: Instrumental Prelude

[3]Congregational Meditation Songs
"As the Deer" *Sing three times*   *NS* 2
"Face to Face"   *NS* 9
"Give Thanks"   *NS* 11

[4]Welcome

[5]Call to Worship: Romans 8:15b-17

*Hymn: "Oh, for a Thousand Tongues to Sing"   *HS* 19

[6]*Prayer of Invocation

*Response

[7]Scripture Lesson: Romans 6:3-4

[8]Words of Challenge and Guidance

[9]Hymn: "Redeeming Grace Has Touched Our Lives" stanza 1   *HS* 351

[10]Statement of Commitment

Hymn: "Redeeming Grace Has Touched Our Lives" stanza 2   *HS* 351

Statement of Commitment

Hymn: "Redeeming Grace Has Touched Our Lives" stanza 3   *HS* 351

[11]Statement of Support to Candidates

Hymn: "Redeeming Grace Has Touched Our Lives" stanza 4   *HS* 351

[12]Sacrament of Baptism
                 Sarah Hernandez by Priest Connie Garcia
                 Herbert Mellenkamp by Elder Burton Smith

[13]Disciples' Generous Response
   Scripture: Doctrine and Covenants 153:9a-b
   Blessing and Offering of Mission Tithes

[14]*Hymn of Blessing: "Rain Down"   *R*-8

[15]*Sending Forth

[16]*Postlude and Greeting of the Newly Baptized

*All who are able may stand.

Our songbooks:
HS=*Hymns of the Saints*, large burgundy book
SP=*Sing for Peace*, small burgundy book
NS=*Sing a New Song*, small gold book
R-x=*By Request: Songs for the Community of Christ*, small book with Temple spire

"Come to the Water"—Annotations

I. The World Church theme and lectionary scripture lessons for the day can often be used in creative and fresh ways to incorporate a sacrament. However, if they do not fit, a theme more directly applicable to baptism can be drawn from scripture or hymnody. Often baptisms are held at a river or lakeside. Bulletins are less common in such circumstances. To those accustomed to bulletins, such services will require attention to verbal instructions that do not interrupt the flow and focus of worship.

2. If possible, a guitar, flute, cello, saxophone, or clarinet would be a fitting instrument to guide the congregation into worship. The same instrument(s) could be used as accompaniment for the three congregational meditation songs that follow.

3. The songs can be sung *to* the congregation, *by* the congregation, or in combination.

4. The welcome is an opportunity to issue an invitation for all to join in worship, with a special welcome to guests. The presider announces the theme and indicates that today's service will focus on the sacrament of baptism.

5. This scripture acknowledges worship as a time when disciples can call out to God as they would to a loving parent. It prepares the congregation to receive the good news that we are the family of God, God's children. It also anticipates the "inheritance" of suffering and of glory to be symbolized in the act of baptism later in the service. A family member of the baptismal candidate might be asked to read the scripture.

6. The purpose of the invocation is to express thanks to God for God's presence and grace, to ask for God's Spirit to touch individuals and the community in life changing ways.

7. The scripture lesson is connected specifically to the theme: "The Dying and the Rising." Many citations can be used to emphasize

other significant meanings of the sacrament of baptism, including Matthew 3:13-17, Mark 1:7-9, John 3:5, Acts 2:37-38, Colossians 2:12, Doctrine and Covenants 17:21, and Mosiah 9:35-42.

8. The eight-to-ten minute challenge to the baptismal candidates and the congregation is based on the scripture lesson. The speaker shares remarks on the nature of the sacrament and a challenge to the congregation and the candidates focusing on the personal commitment of the candidate and the corporate responsibility to support and nurture new disciples.

9. The stanzas of the baptismal hymn on which the theme is based are used to highlight statements of commitment by the candidates and congregational representative.

10. Each candidate makes a statement of personal commitment.

11. Ask a representative of the congregation to make a pledge of support to the baptismal candidates.

12. Before each baptism, the names of the candidate and officiating minister are announced. Instrumental music is appropriate for meditation as the candidates and ministers enter and leave the water.

13. An offering is appropriate if it takes place as a part of regular congregational worship. It is often not included when the baptism is held on another occasion or outside the congregational building. The scripture provides opportunity for the person giving the thoughts and prayer on the offering to build on the connection between tithes, church mission, and the call to invite others to be baptized.

14. This hymn from *By Request: Songs for the Community of Christ* affirms God's generosity—a helpful follow-up to the offertory. It alludes once again to the symbol of water so central to the sacrament of baptism. It also petitions God for love, hope, protection, and peace as we depart.

15. The presider closes the worship by sending forth the baptismal candidates and all gathered disciples. In a brief declaration she or he assures them of God's faithfulness and calls them to be faithful to God's call to love the world and to make new disciples within their spheres of influence.

16. In some jurisdictions it is customary to greet the candidate with an embrace and words of congratulations and support as the worship participants part from the baptismal setting.

The Gift of God's Spirit
A Celebration of the Sacrament
of Confirmation

[2]Prelude and Gathering

Congregational Song of Invitation: "Holy Spirit, Come with Power" *HS* 287

[3]Lighting the Peace Candle

[4]Welcome and Scriptural Call to Worship: Acts 1:6-8

*Hymn: "O God, to Us Be Present Here"   *HS* 358

[5]*Invocation of the Holy Spirit

*Response

Disciples' Generous Response
> Reflection: God's Spirit moves in and among us. What is our response? We have been given blessings that enable us to be generous and share financially to meet our local needs as well as the ministry we can provide to a needy world.

> Blessing and Offering of Mission Tithes

[6]Ministry of Music: "O Lord, We Come As Children All"   *HS* 360

[7]Scripture Reading: Galatians 5:22-23, 25

[8]Confirmation Sermon: "Spirit, Power, and Blessing"

[9]Hymn of Preparation: "Lay Your Hands"   *NS* 27

[10]The Sacrament of Confirmation

[11]Circle of Support

[12]*Hymn of Blessing: "Go, My Children"   *SP* 44

*Benediction

*Response

*Postlude

---

*All who are able may stand.

Our songbooks:
> *HS*=*Hymns of the Saints*, large burgundy book
> *SP*=*Sing for Peace*, small burgundy book
> *NS*=*Sing a New Song*, small gold book
> *R-x*=*By Request: Songs for the Community of Christ*, small book with Temple spire

"The Gift of God's Spirit"—Annotations

1. If a printed order of worship is used, create a heading that lists the theme and focus of the service.
2. Announcements should be made before the prelude. At the conclusion of the announcements, the congregation is requested to begin a period of quiet reflection as the music minister plays a prelude.
3. In congregations that have a tradition of lighting a peace candle, the candle is lit either during the singing of the hymn or at its conclusion. If the congregation prays specifically for a different nation each week, this would be the time to include the prayer.
4. The presider calls the congregation to worship and makes remarks that focus on the Holy Spirit. He or she informs the people that the sacrament of confirmation will be celebrated. The presider welcomes those present and concludes with the scripture reading from Acts.
5. The invocation is one of thanksgiving, praise, and recognition of the impact of the Holy Spirit on the lives of God's people.
6. The ministry of music (HS 360) could be sung by a solo voice, accompanied by piano/keyboard and, if possible, one other instrument— drum, finger cymbal, or other simple percussion instrument.
7. The reading could be delivered by the confirmation candidate or other member of the congregation. It could also be read in several languages.
8. The ten-minute sermon focuses on the implications of living life in the Spirit, using the apostle Paul's Galatian letter as the basis for the remarks. It speaks to what others will evidence in and through us.
9. During the hymn of preparation, the candidate(s) and officiating elders take their places in the front of the sanctuary. If desired, the presider may announce the participants' names before the sacrament.
10. Two elders place their hands on the head of the candidate as one offers the prayer of confirmation. Consider whether the spokesperson needs to use a microphone so that everyone can hear. The prayer should be addressed to God, not the candidate, and should include recognition of the gift of the Holy Spirit and entrance into membership in the Community of Christ.
11. After the confirmation prayer, the congregation is invited to form a circle around the newly confirmed. The pastor or other leader then makes a statement of welcome and support, and gives the new member a small gift (*Walking with Jesus: A Member's Guide in the Community of Christ* is available from Herald House), membership certificate, or some other symbol from the congregation.
12. The congregation remains in a circle as it sings the closing hymn and the final prayer is offered.

Come to the Table of Jesus
Sacrament of Communion

Worship Setting: The Communion table begins empty. Have a loaf of bread on a plate, a pitcher of grape juice, and a candle ready to be carried to the table, along with the prepared emblems during the introit.

[1]Introit

[2]*Invocation

*Invocation Hymn: "O Lord, Grace Our Communion"   *HS* 1

[3]Reading of the Scriptures

    Luke 22:7-20
    John 6:35-40
    John 8:12

Hymn of Repentance: "The Love of God"   *HS* 107

[4]Silent Prayers of Confession

[5]Prayer of Repentance

[6]Communion Message

Hymn of Preparation: "For Bread Before Us Broken"   *HS* 340

The Lord's Supper
    Blessing and Serving of the Bread
       [7]Ministry of Music
    Blessing and Serving of the Wine
       Ministry of Music

[8]Testimony of God's Forgiving Love

Disciples' Generous Response
    Oblation Scripture: Isaiah 61:1-2a
    Reflection: On the first Sunday of the month we emphasize the needs in our world and encourage the generous donation of oblation funds. This is one way we can bring the good news to those in need. We are also encouraged by the Isaiah scripture to look beyond the physical needs to help the oppressed, brokenhearted, and captives. May we be generous with all that we are.
    Blessing and Offering of Oblation/Mission Tithes

*Benediction Hymn: "Called by Christ to Love Each Other"   *SP* 36

*Prayer of Blessing

[9]*Sending Forth and Recessional

---

*All who are able may stand.

98

Our songbooks:

   HS=Hymns of the Saints, large burgundy book
   SP=Sing for Peace, small burgundy book
   NS=Sing a New Song, small gold book
   R-x=By Request: Songs for the Community of Christ, small book with Temple spire

"Come to the Table of Jesus"—Annotations

1. The music suggested for the introit is a solo voice, singing (perhaps a cappella) a text of invitation to the table. Some suggestions include: "Be Present at Our Table, Lord," *HS* 336; "Come, Risen Lord," *HS* 344; "Gather Your Children," *SP* 3; "Meet Me in a Holy Place," *NS* 36; "Face to Face," *NS* 9.

   During the introit carry a lighted candle, then the loaf of bread on a plate, from the back to the front of the sanctuary. Have others follow carrying the plates of broken bread. Next, carry the pitcher of grape juice followed by the trays. Place the candle, loaf of bread, and pitcher of juice in the center of the Communion table. Place the plates and trays around these items. This is intended to help the congregation experience gathering around the table. The candle represents the light and life of Jesus.

2. After the introit, ask the congregation to stand for the invocation.

3. Ask three people to read the scriptures. Use a variety of ages.

4. Invite the congregation to spend one-to-two minutes in silent prayers of confession. This may be an uncomfortable amount of time for some, but the officiants on the rostrum can set an example for the congregation.

5. Ask a representative of the congregation to voice a public prayer of confession and repentance.

6. Focus the message on the experience of Jesus with the disciples around the table. What does it mean to be invited to this table of Jesus? How can our lives be changed?

7. Ask the minister of music to sing or play songs that reflect God's love, mercy, and forgiveness while the emblems are served. Some suggestions include: "My Shepherd Will Supply My Need," *HS* 125; "Forgive Our Sins as We Forgive," *HS* 108; "Gather Your Children," *SP* 3; "Hosea," *NS* 15.

8. Ask someone to share a testimony of how the sacrament of the Lord's Supper has changed them and made life different.

9. Have the people who carried the candle, loaf of bread, and pitcher of juice carry these items out of the sanctuary. Invite the congregation to follow them out, symbolizing carrying the light of Jesus out into the world and bringing food to those who are hungry.

I Have Called You by Your Name
Sacrament of Ordination

Prelude

[1]Welcome and Call to Discipleship

Gathering Hymn: "Touch Me, Lord, with Thy Spirit Eternal"   *HS* 409

Call to Worship: Doctrine and Covenants 162:1b, 2a–c

*Hymn of Petition: "Help Us Express Your Love"   *HS* 415

*Invocation

*Response

[2]Focus Moment: "Samuel Hears God's Call"

Disciples' Generous Response
    Scripture: Doctrine and Covenants 162:7c–d
    Blessing and Offering of Mission Tithes
    Giving Hymn: "Community of Christ"   *R*-14

[3]Testimony of Ministry

Servant Hymn: "I Have Called You by Your Name" stanza 1   *R*-10

[4]Call to Ordination

Servant Hymn: "I Have Called You by Your Name" stanza 2   *R*-10

[5]Testimony of Response

Servant Hymn: "I Have Called You by Your Name" stanza 3   *R*-10

[6]Ordination Prayer

Servant Hymn: "I Have Called You by Your Name" stanza 4   *R*-10

[7]Testimony of Receiving

[8]Pastoral Prayer

*Going Forth Hymn: "Take the Path of the Disciple"   *R*-19

*Postlude

---

*All who are able may stand.

Our songbooks:
    HS=*Hymns of the Saints*, large burgundy book
    SP=*Sing for Peace*, small burgundy book
    NS=*Sing a New Song*, small gold book
    R-x=*By Request: Songs for the Community of Christ*, small book with Temple spire

"I Have Called You by Your Name"—Annotations

1. Welcome and invite all to worship. Also articulate the call of each person to discipleship, reminding us that we are all called to offer ministry in the congregation and the community.

2. Share the story of young Samuel found in I Samuel, chapters 1-3. Use a children's Bible for a condensed version of the story. Samuel (and Hannah) answered God's call. What are some of the ways we hear God's call today? How do we answer God's call?

3. Invite a person who holds the same priesthood office as the one being ordained to share a testimony about the ministry of this office of priesthood. How has the Spirit blessed his or her ministry? How has priesthood responsibility caused him or her to grow?

4. This is the sermon. Include a discussion of the particular priesthood office of the ordinand and the needs it fulfills within the body of Christ. Challenge the ordinand to offer his/her gifts in ministry. Challenge the congregation to offer support and help to the ordinand. Affirm God's call to people of every era to be in the midst of the people as ministers.

5. Ask the ordinand to share his or her testimony of accepting this call and hopes for ministry.

6. If desired, the presider may announce the participants' names before the ordination.

7. Invite a representative of the congregation to affirm the call and response of the person just ordained, offering the help and support of the congregation in this new ministry.

8. If possible, form a circle around the perimeter of the sanctuary before this prayer is offered.

We Seek Wholeness
Healing Service

Prelude

²Welcome

Call to Worship: Psalm 130

³*Songs

"Holy Ground"	*NS* 13
"Come, Holy Spirit, Come"	*NS* 6

⁴*Invocation

⁵Meditation Reading: Psalm 139:1-14

⁶The Lord's Prayer

Song: "I Love You, Lord"   *NS* 18

⁷Scriptural Example of Healing: Acts 3:1-10

Song of Praise: "Hosanna"   *NS* 14

⁸Presentation of the Oil

Song of Petition: "Jesus, Remember Me"   *NS* 26

⁹Invitation to Administration / Prayers for Wholeness

Ministry of Music: "Face to Face"   *NS* 9

¹⁰Prayer Time

*Song of Affirmation: "Santo, Santo, Santo"   *NS* 43

*Benediction

_____

*All who are able may stand.

Our songbooks:
    HS=Hymns of the Saints, large burgundy book
    SP=Sing for Peace, small burgundy book
    NS=Sing a New Song, small gold book
    R-x=By Request: Songs for the Community of Christ, small book with Temple spire

"We Seek Wholeness"—Annotations

1. This service is based on the worship style of the Taizé community in France, founded in 1940. It may be appropriate to announce the worship service as a healing service, rather than a Taizé worship, to avoid confusion over the meaning of the name. The worship style can then be explained in the introduction. Information on the Taizé community and worship resources can be found on the Internet (in many languages) at *http://www.taize.fr/*, or from a Christian bookstore or library.

   Usually Taizé chants are sung without printed words, as they are repetitive and the congregation can quickly learn them. Depending on the setting and the congregation, a choir can be used to introduce the chant, with the congregation invited to join in after a couple of repetitions. There are audio samples of Taizé songs available on the Internet (*http://www.taize.fr/en/en_article681.html?var_recherche=audio+sample*) and on CD.

   Attention must be given to the worship setting. Subdued lighting and candles may assist in creating a safe and sacred space for congregational participation. This style of worship service is more powerful when the people are informed beforehand as to the purpose of the worship. An optimum occasion would be an evening service, especially during a reunion experience. This is intended to be a healing service, where people come forward without prior request, for prayers of administration, and an invitation can also be given for people to come forward and kneel to offer silent prayers.

2. The presider welcomes the congregation and explains the flow of the service, preparing those present for the invitation to come for prayers of administration later in the service. An explanation of Taizé worship can be included.

3. During the singing, it may be helpful to have a song leader, as the songs are usually repeated, and volume of the singing may be increased or decreased according to the direction of the leader.

4. The opening prayer includes an invocation of God's Spirit. It may contain statements of praise and thanksgiving, preparing the people to be present and aware of the presence of God's Spirit. The prayer could be given in a language other than the usual language of the congregation (for example, a prayer in French in an English-speaking congregation) to remind the people to listen to the voice of the Spirit, rather than just the words of the prayer.

5. Use several readers for this scripture with a variety of voice timbres.

6. The Lord's Prayer can be shared by the congregation, as printed in the *Hymns of the Saints*, or offered in a variety of languages (*www.christusrex.org/www1/pater/* has the prayer in more than a thousand languages). Time can also be allowed for personal silent prayer. Taizé worship

usually includes five-to-ten minutes of silent prayer.

7. Have two people (Peter and the beggar) act out the scripture as it is read.

8. The oil for the anointing during the administration may be shown ceremonially to the congregation (for example, one elder holding the container or bottle of oil) while another elder offers a prayer or statement of blessing, consecrating the oil in the presence of the congregation.

9. Provide guidance as to how the administrations will occur. Brief statements on the meaning of administration, including an explanation of the use of the oil, and the two prayers (anointing and blessing) are recommended. The people are invited to contemplate their need for prayer during the ministry of music and prepare to come forward to be seated in one of the chairs at the front of the sanctuary to receive administration.

The congregation is invited to offer silent prayers for those seeking administration, so they are actively engaged in the healing service. This is part of the call to community, to support each other in times of need.

10. Following the ministry of music, a brief statement of invitation is made, so the congregation knows now is the time for them to come forward if they seek administration.

The selection of the elders to perform these administrations must be undertaken prayerfully and with consideration of their spiritual maturity. They may be asked to pray for people they do not know, relying on the guidance of the Spirit.

The number of chairs and elders available will depend on the size of the congregation. In one worship setting, four chairs were placed at the front of the sanctuary, facing forward, rather than facing the congregation. Eight elders took their places behind the chairs, facing the cross at the front of the sanctuary, and the administrations were done one at a time. In other situations the administration prayers can be offered concurrently, quietly audible to the candidate.

Invite the congregation to come forward to light small candles and offer silent prayers at the front of the sanctuary, either in place of receiving administration or in addition. This movement of people has several purposes: it allows people a chance to move, rather than sitting throughout the prayer time; it may give people more confidence to come forward for administration; and the candles enhance the worship setting. Quiet background music would be appropriate during the prayer time. The intent of offering the administrations in this way is to make them public yet private and freely available to all.

The prayer time concludes when there are no more coming forward for administration and all have completed their private prayers at the front of the sanctuary.

The Sacrament of Marriage
Uniting
Samantha Smith
and
Jonathon Jones

[2]Prelude and Seating of the Guests

[3]Statement of Purpose

[4]Processional: "Trumpet Voluntary"   Jeremiah Clarke

[5]Minister's Welcome

[6]Prayer of Invocation

[7]Reading of the Scripture: I Corinthians 13

Congregational Hymn: "Every Good and Perfect Gift"   HS 151

[8]Charge to the Bride and Bridegroom

[9]Reading and Lighting of the Candles

[10]The Exchange of Vows and Rings

[11]Prayer of Blessing

[12]Pronouncement and Presentation of the Couple

[13]Recessional: "Trumpet Tune"   Purcell

The Sacrament of Marriage—Annotations

1. This sacrament service should be sacred in nature. Secular readings and songs are not appropriate during the service, but could be shared during the wedding reception or another part of the celebration.

2. The guests and family members are seated during the playing of the prelude, with the parents usually seated just before the beginning of the ceremony. The instrument used is often organ, piano, or a small string ensemble. Commonly chosen pieces include Pachelbel's "Canon in D" and J.S. Bach's "Jesu, Joy of Man's Desiring."

3. The Statement of Purpose is delivered by the officiating minister as a brief welcome and explanation to the congregation. It emphasizes

that those gathered are now a specially assembled congregation, diverse in many ways, but united in their support of the bride and groom. Invite the congregation to participate as witnesses, and to realize that for the next few moments they are engaged in worship. Remind the congregation that all worship, including weddings, is *God-centered.*

4. The wedding processional usually includes the bride and bridegroom, along with their attendants. If several people are involved, it is wise to rehearse the processional. Indeed, many couples now choose to have a rehearsal of the entire ceremony, often on the day before. Manuals on weddings will often contain sample processionals and ways to organize the wedding party.

5. The minister now has opportunity to welcome the wedding party and the congregation, and to make a statement about the nature and purpose of the sacrament and the couple's wish to make a covenant with God and one another.

6. The opening prayer includes an invocation of God's Spirit. It may contain statements of praise and thanksgiving. It should not be a prayer of blessing, which comes later in the ceremony.

7. The entirety of I Corinthians 13 is read. A contemporary language version of the text, such as the New Revised Standard Version, may be easier for the congregation to understand.

8. The minister delivers a five-to-ten-minute homily. It contains counsel to the couple, which could include the following:

   Serve as one another's advocate

   Accept each other as a gift from God

   Establish a Christian home of joy

   Treat one another with mutual regard

   Learn to speak honestly and openly with each other

   Develop a spiritual life together

   Recognize that marriage is a journey that is not always easy

   Constantly seek a deeper meaning and relationship

9. If the couple chooses, the ceremony could include a special reading and/or lighting of candles placed in the front of the church. The reader(s) could be selected family or friends, and the candle lighting might also include the parents or other significant people in the lives of the bride and groom.

10. The exchange of vows in the Community of Christ should include

Doctrine and Covenants 111:2b. This can be artistically placed at the end of other statements of vows. The vows made by the man are to be identical or very similar to those made by the woman, without gender distinction. They can be repeated in short phrases, first stated by the minister, or delivered directly by the bride and bridegroom. Some couples may choose to write their own vows.

The rings can be exchanged at the conclusion of the vows or incorporated into the vows by using a statement like, "With this ring, I promise to..."

11. The minister offers a pastoral prayer of blessing on the lives of the bride and groom. This blessing is a significant point in a religious wedding that does not and cannot occur in a civil marriage ceremony.

12. The minister officially declares the couple married by words such as, "By the authority given me as a minister within the Community of Christ and by the laws of this state, I pronounce you a married couple, husband and wife." The pronouncement may be followed by the couple exchanging a kiss.

    At this point, in the United Kingdom and Australia, for example, legal documents may be signed in accordance with the law of the land.

    In many cases, it is traditional for the newly married couple to face the congregation as the minister ends with words such as, "Dear family and friends, it is with the greatest of pleasure that I present to you Samantha and Jonathon Jones." No attempt should be made to prevent the congregation from applauding at this juncture.

13. The wedding recessional features a jubilant piece of music or congregational hymn. The bride and groom recess first, followed by the wedding party. Be sure the ushers have been instructed on the mechanics of dismissing the congregation.

The Vision of a Life to Be
Sacramental Blessing of a Child

Prelude

Songs of Praise: "Sing a New Song"   NS 1
                 "God of the Sparrow"   SP 13

Words of Welcome and Call to Worship: Psalm 8:1-5

*Hymn of Invitation: "Come, Rejoice Before Your Maker"   HS 44

*Prayer of Thanksgiving

*Response

Disciples' Generous Response
      Scripture: Doctrine and Covenants 162:7a
      Blessing and Offering of Mission Tithes

Focus Moment: "The Miracle of You"

Ministry of Music: "The Vision of a Life to Be"   HS 349

Scripture Lesson: Mark 10:13-16

Sermon on the Blessing of a Child

Hymn of Preparation: "We Bring Our Children, Lord, to Thee"   HS 348

Sacrament of Blessing
                          Allison Erin Parker
                  Daughter of Aaron and Courtney Parker
                            will be blessed by
                Elders Breanne Thompson and Luke Peltier

Congregational Response

*Hymn of Blessing: "I Have Called You by Your Name"   R-10

*Closing Prayer

*Postlude

---

*All who are able may stand.

Our songbooks:
    HS=*Hymns of the Saints*, large burgundy book
    SP=*Sing for Peace*, small burgundy book
    NS=*Sing a New Song*, small gold book
    R-x=*By Request: Songs for the Community of Christ*, small book with Temple spire

"The Vision of a Life to Be"—Annotations

1. Make every attempt to use the World Church theme and lectionary scriptures for the day. If they do not seem appropriate for the sacrament, select a theme and scriptures that highlight the blessing of children.

2. Announcements should be made before the prelude. After announcements, the congregation is invited to a time of reflection and preparation for worship as the musical prelude is offered.

3. A song leader invites the congregation to make an offering of praise to God in song. Though many songs and hymns are appropriate, these are offered to focus on the "new" and "creation" in preparation for celebrating the birth and blessing of a child.

4. The presider warmly welcomes the congregation to this sacred time and space. He or she informs participants that they will share in a sacrament of blessing of a child. (It is, of course, appropriate to bless more than one child in such a service. Only slight adjustments would need to be made to the program.) The presider either reads, or invites the congregation to read in unison, this psalm about "divine majesty and human dignity."

5. This hymn is an invitation to all to "Come before the Creator." It is especially appropriate to the blessing of children in the assurance that God's faithfulness endures *to every generation* (stanza 4).

6. The prayer is a humble expression of thanksgiving, praise, and trust in the Creator and Sustainer, whom we worship.

7. The offertory statement and prayer provide an opportunity to invite the congregation to tangibly express generosity to the children of the earth, and that joy may increase and grace abound throughout the world, not simply for the one child who will be blessed in the congregation this day. The children of the congregation may be invited to receive the offering.

8. The Focus Moment should not be used as a time to speak about the sacrament of blessing. That will be done by the speaker later in the service. Show in pictures, sonograms, video clips, etc., the miracle of new life and the amazing potential that resides within those tiny, fragile, intricate creatures (human or animal). Share the uniqueness of every creature. Point out unique aspects of some people in the congregation, ending with something unique about the baby(ies) about to be blessed. Each of us is God's miracle!

9. This is a beautiful child-blessing hymn written by Geoffrey F. Spencer (*HS* 349) from which the theme for the service is drawn. It can be sung as a solo or by a trio or quartet, either accompanied or a cappella. Alternatively, a children's choir could offer this ministry of music.

10. Additional scripture readings would include the following: Matthew 19:13-15; Luke 18:15-17; Mosiah 2:25, 27; III Nephi 8:23; Doctrine and Covenants 17:19.

11. The eight-to-ten-minute message could include reflection on the inestimable worth of one human being, the potential resident within this new life, the purpose and significance of the sacrament of blessing. It is also appropriate to speak to the parents and family, thanking them for bringing the child for blessing, impressing upon them their responsibilities, as well as challenging the congregation to help nurture and teach the child as he or she grows. It is always appropriate to acknowledge the love and blessing of God as creator and sustainer of the child.

12. It is appropriate to announce the blessing of the child before or immediately following the singing of the congregational hymn of preparation. Announce the name of the child, the names of the parents, and the names of those who will perform the sacrament. The parents, and possibly other significant family members—brothers and sisters, for example—bring the child forward to a designated place as the last verse of the hymn is sung. The child is given to the elder who will assist in the blessing.

13. The prayer should be brief and loud enough for all to hear. It is desirable that the elder use the name of the child in the prayer of blessing. The blessing represents a covenant entered into by the parents (or guardian), the congregation, and God. It is an opportunity to acknowledge God's love and concern for the child, to recognize the uniqueness and worth of the child, to confess our human dependence on God, and to request God's care for the child and provision of the Holy Spirit as guide and strength.

14. The congregational response could include one of the following: a statement/testimony by a congregational representative promising love and support to the child and parents; a written statement to the child by each member of the congregation that could be bound in a small book and given to the family in a follow-up visit to the home by the pastor, or the elders who performed the sacrament; the presentation of a small gift to the family from the congregation, symbolizing the privilege and challenge of Christian parenthood. Or, the response might be by a sibling, grandparent, or parent who articulates how they see God reflected in the face of this child; or what vision and hope they have for this child's life.

15. Though this hymn is not specific to baby blessings, it is most appropriate. We are told that God knows each of us by name, that we belong to God, that God will not abandon us, that God will help us learn God's name as we grow.

16. The brief closing prayer thanks God for abundant grace and asks a blessing as the congregation departs to tell all God's precious children they belong to God.

[1] Love as I Have Loved You
A Service of Congregational Blessing

[2] Prelude and Preparation

[3] Hymn of Gathering: "Gather Your Children" stanzas 1 and 2   SP 3

[4] Lighting of the Peace Candle and Prayer for Peace

[5] Welcome

[6] Call to Worship: I Peter 3:8-12

*Hymn: "Holy Spirit, Come with Power"   HS 287

[7] *Prayer of Invocation

*Response

Disciples' Generous Response
> Reflection: What is our response as followers of Jesus? How will we extend this blessing to others?
> Blessing and Offering of Mission Tithes

[8] Scripture Reading and Homily

[9] Hymn: "Weave"   NS 51

[10] Testimony of Harmony

[11] Hymn: "Mighty God, Transforming God!" stanza 1   NS 38

[12] Testimony of Transformation and Empowerment

[13] Song of Dedication: "Lord I Give You" stanzas 1-3   NS 32

[14] Blessing of the Priesthood
Blessing of the Children and Youth

Song of Dedication: "Lord, I Give You" stanzas 4-7   NS 32

> Blessing of the Families and Home
> Blessing of the Congregation

[15] *Hymn: "Gather Your Children" stanzas 3 and 4   SP 3

*Sending Forth
> Go forth, blessed to be a blessing to others: "Love as I Have Loved You." Amen.

*Postlude

---

*All who are able may stand.

Our songbooks:
> HS=*Hymns of the Saints*, large burgundy book
> SP=*Sing for Peace*, small burgundy book
> NS=*Sing a New Song*, small gold book
> R-x=*By Request: Songs for the Community of Christ*, small book with Temple spire

"Love as I Have Loved You"—Annotations

Congregational Blessing

As with all orders of worship in which a sacrament is enacted, the congregational blessing should be the liturgy's focal point or climax. The welcome, call to worship, invocation, scripture readings, hymns, and homily should thematically complement the purpose of the service and move the worshipers in a meaningful way toward participation in the blessing. Accordingly, the blessing should not be given early in the service.

The congregational blessing is ideally a culmination of many weeks of dialogue, home visitation, priesthood and leadership meetings, and other congregational activities focused on a congregation's particular need. The blessing should address the need and should be contextual to all age groups.

1. Make every attempt to use the World Church theme and lectionary scriptures for the day. If they do not seem appropriate for the sacrament, select a theme and scriptures that highlight the sacrament of blessing.

2. Through music and, perhaps, presider's comments, the congregation is encouraged to gather in a manner that allows for preparation for the sacrament.

3. The gathering hymn properly reflects the anticipation of the congregation in being together for the celebration of the sacrament.

4. If your congregation has the tradition of lighting a peace candle and offering the prayer for peace, include it here.

5. The presider should warmly welcome all attendees and briefly address the unique purpose of this service, particularly for the benefit of visitors.

6. The suggested call to worship scripture focuses on harmony.

7. The prayer of invocation can include a statement of thanksgiving, praise, and expectation, as well as invoking God's Spirit.

8. For this service, the reading and homily are not the focal point of the worship and should be much briefer than a typical sermon. Five minutes are sufficient. The homily should address the scriptural theme and prepare the congregation for the blessing to follow.

9. A hymn of unity and purpose fits the focus of the worship and the sacrament.

10. The testimony should also be brief and focus solely on the image of harmony.

11. This hymn could be omitted or replaced by a ministry of music. It could also be changed to a brief period of silence.

12. See note 10, only this time the image is of transformation and empowerment.

13. The song of dedication is broken into segments and allows the congregation to participate as community in the midst of the blessing.

14. There is no prescribed formula for the prayer of blessing. Although this order of worship illustrates the evangelist's blessing as three separate prayers, this should not be understood to be the preferred model for this unique sacrament. The blessing can be offered by one evangelist or more than one. If there are several prayers, they can each have a central focus, as in this order of worship. A basic outline for a prayer of blessing is as follows:

    Salutation: The salutation addresses God. It includes praise and thanksgiving and functions much like an invocation.

    Purpose: The blessing's central purpose should be stated early in the prayer.

    Petition: A petition for God's blessing should be contextual to the age groups and families represented.

    Congregation's Covenant: This is an expression of the congregation's commitment to work toward the desired focus (mission, reconciliation, healing, etc.).

    God's Covenant: The evangelist should articulate God's desire and willingness to bless the congregation. This is where specific words of counsel and guidance are offered. This is the central body of the prayer—an expression of God's longing to strengthen the group as an authentic community of Jesus Christ.

    Conclusion: The evangelist concludes quickly and briefly with a closing statement and amen.

15. Ask the congregation to form a circle around the perimeter of the sanctuary before singing the remaining stanzas of this hymn.

Embracing Loss and Promise
Memorial Service

[1]Prelude

Gathering of Family and Friends

[2]Creating Life Center

[3]Words of Welcome and Compassion

[4]Gathering Prayer

[5]Prayer Response: "Heal Me, Hands of Jesus" stanza 1   *SP* 33

[6]Scripture Reading

    Psalm 130:1-2, 5-6

    I Corinthians 15:55-57

    Romans 14:7-9

    Romans 8:35, 37-39

    II Nephi 1:72

    Doctrine and Covenants 22:23b

[7]Hymn: "God! When Human Bonds Are Broken"   *SP* 18

[8]Selected Readings

[9]Ministry of Music: "O Love That Wilt Not Let Me Go"   *HS* 132

[10]Words of Promise and Hope

[11]Sharing Remembrances

[12]Hymn: "O God, Our Help in Ages Past"   *HS* 200

[13]Pastoral Prayer

[14]Recessional

Our songbooks:
    HS=*Hymns of the Saints,* large burgundy book
    SP=*Sing for Peace,* small burgundy book
    NS=*Sing a New Song,* small gold book
    R-x=*By Request: Songs for the Community of Christ,* small book with Temple spire

Words of Hope
Graveside Service

[1]Words of Gathering

[2]Sharing Scriptures

[3]Words of Assurance

[4]Prayer

[5]Expressions of Friendship

"Embracing Loss and Promise"—Annotations

1. Use hymns and songs that are meaningful to the family of the deceased, perhaps including the favorite hymns of the deceased. If there is not an organ or piano available, recorded music may be used.

2. Ask members of the family, before they are seated, to bring items that represent their loved one to the worship center at the front of the sanctuary. These items provide the worship center for the service, a visual comfort and remembrance for the family and friends. Each person could also share the significance of the item, if desired.

3. Offer words of welcome in God's name and on behalf of the family. Invite the gathered into God's arms of peace and compassion. Include God's loving awareness of the pain and tears and invite all to worship together in loving memory of the deceased.

4. Prayer for the family and friends who have gathered, asking God to bless them with peace and comfort.

5. As a musical response to the prayer, this stanza is sung as a solo.

6. Use several or all of the suggested scriptures. These words reflect our human grief and longing.

7. If the service does not include congregational singing, this hymn could be sung as a ministry of music. An alternative hymn suggestion is "Lord, in This Hour" *HS* 150.

8. Choose readings that are special and meaningful to the family. Use readers from the extended family and friends of the deceased. The following resources may be helpful.

   Sourcebook of Funerals, Volume 1 and 2; Communication Resources, Inc., Canton, Ohio; ISBN 0-930921-13-5 and 0-930921-18-6.

   Psalms of Lament by Ann Weems; Westminster John Knox Press, Louisville, Kentucky; ISBN 0-664-22074-6.

Lament for a Son by Nicholas Wolterstorff; William B. Eerdmans Publishing Company, Grand Rapids, Michigan; ISBN 0-8028-0294-X.

Deeper Than Tears; Word Publishing, Dallas, Texas; ISBN 0-8499-1496-5.

Your Sorrow Is My Sorrow by Joyce Rupp; The Crossroad Publishing Company, New York, New York; ISBN 0-8245-1566-8.

9. This hymn could be sung by a quartet or as a solo.

10. This is the sermon or homily. Reflect on the scriptures and readings that have been used in the service or select others. Acknowledge the loss and offer comfort, hope, the promise of God's abiding love, the light and life of Jesus, and the promise of life eternal. This is not the time to offer words that will comfort hearts in the days to come. This is not the time to "preach," but to assure the congregation of the promise and hope of the message of Jesus and the love of God.

11. Invite members of the family or friends to share memories of the deceased or ask that they write down the memories to be read aloud by the minister. Also, if there is time, the congregation could be asked to share memories.

12. If the service does not include congregational singing, this hymn could be sung as a ministry of music.

13. Pray for the family in the days and months ahead; for their healing; for remembered memories; for others in attendance to remember the family in their grief; for God to hold them and bless them with peace, hope, promise, and love.

14. Music is provided as the service ends. Be sure to review with the ushers the mechanics of the family leaving and then the congregation.

Note: If asked to do a memorial service for a child, teenager, or young adult, it is important to use more words and thoughts that acknowledge the loss and the family's grief. The family and friends may be experiencing deep anger, shock, and denial and will need others, especially the minister, to understand their feelings and to offer God's love and tears in a very deep and abiding way and to find profound words for assuring life eternal.

"Words of Hope"—Annotations

1. Begin the graveside service with words acknowledging the sadness, yet knowing that the deceased now lives with God and is in the welcoming and loving arms of the Almighty. Include assurance of eternal life: in the dark night of sorrow, the light and life of Jesus has gifted the deceased with a special place prepared for him or her. Sorrow is enfolded by the hope and promise found in the life of Jesus Christ.

2. Suggestions include the following: John 11:25, 26; John 14:27; I Corinthians 15:54; Isaiah 41:13; I John 4:9; I Corinthians 15:57.

3. This should be five or six sentences of assurance and hope. Reflect on the scriptures and include words of comfort and assurance to help the family leave their loved one. Affirm that this life prepares us for the next perfect life within God's realm.

4. Pray family and friends as they now go home with an emptiness and loss so fresh and real. Pray for peace, mercy, and the love of God to comfort and sustain them.

5. The minister should go first to the family and then to others offering a hand or embrace, wishing each God's love and care.

APPENDIX
Implementation of World Conference Resolution 1282: Prayers for the Sacrament of the Lord's Supper

By the First Presidency

The sacraments of the church are essential expressions of our unity as a worldwide fellowship. Sacramental practice that provides for using essentially the same forms and words churchwide (albeit in various languages) reinforces a sense of togetherness in the context of wide diversity.

We interpret the intent of World Conference Resolution 1282, approved on April 3, 2004, as calling for the preparation of alternate prayers that retain the overall structure and content of those found in Section 17 of the Doctrine and Covenants. In this way the churchwide use of common forms and wording is preserved.

In recent years, some Communion services have provided for the wine to be served immediately following the bread. This is done either as the servers take the emblems to the congregation or as the congregation comes forward to receive. Where this is done, the reading of two separate prayers, one right after the other, can be awkward. For this reason, we believe that the needs of the church will be well served by having a combined prayer that can be used when the emblems are served together. Such prayers, one using the Doctrine and Covenants language and the other the more contemporary wording, are also provided at this time.

The resolution calls for use of "contemporary language." The attempt has been to replace archaic language with wording that is in current use; this includes gender-specific references to God.

In providing alternate Communion prayers for use in the church, these new prayers will have equal status to those found in Section 17 of the Doctrine and Covenants. In Communion services of the Community of Christ, these two sets of prayers (and their equivalent translations in other languages) are the only ones authorized for use. Those appointed to read the prayers are not free to use other wording.

The following prayers are now offered for use in the church, in addition to those found in Doctrine and Covenants 17: 22 and 23.

Blessing on the Bread

Eternal God, we ask you in the name of your Son Jesus Christ, to bless and sanctify this bread to the souls of all those who receive it, that they may eat in remembrance of the body of your Son, and witness to you, O God, that they are willing to take upon them the name of your Son, and always remember him, and keep the commandments which he has given them, that they may always have his Spirit to be with them. Amen.

Blessing on the Wine

Eternal God, we ask you in the name of your Son Jesus Christ, to bless and sanctify this wine to the souls of all those who receive it, that they may drink in remembrance of the blood of your Son which was shed for them, that they may witness to you, O God, that they do always remember him, that they may have his Spirit to be with them. Amen.

Combined Prayer on the Bread and Wine (from Doctrine and Covenants 17)

O God, the eternal Father, we ask thee in the name of thy Son Jesus Christ, to bless and sanctify this bread and wine to the souls of all those who partake of them, that they may eat and drink in remembrance of the body and blood of thy Son, and witness unto thee, O God, the eternal Father, that they are willing to take upon them the name of thy Son, and always remember him and keep his commandments which he has given them, that they may always have his Spirit to be with them. Amen.

Combined Prayer on the Bread and Wine (contemporary language)

Eternal God, we ask you in the name of your Son Jesus Christ, to bless and sanctify this bread and wine to the souls of all those who receive them, that they may eat and drink in remembrance of the body and blood of your Son, and witness to you, O God, that they are willing to take upon them the name of your Son, and always remember him and keep the commandments which he has given them, that they may always have his Spirit to be with them. Amen.

(September 2004)